Also by Julian Lynn

Four Gates to Health

Divine Fruit

Yoga's Devotional Light

Julian Lynn

Nymphaea Works • Springfield, Missouri

Yoga's Devotional Light

Living Your Bhakti Practice

Author: Julian Lynn
Photographer: Julian Lynn

Cataloging-in-Publication Data
Lynn, Julian
   Yoga's devotional light: living your bhakti practice. / Julian Lynn. -1st ed.

   ISBN 978-0-692-94271-0

   1. Spiritual life. 2. Bhakti yoga. 3. Ethics.
I. Lynn, Julian. II. Title.

2017913479

Dewey-Decimal-System Classification: 294

questions@julianlynn.com

Copyright © 2017 Julian Lynn

The text and photographic works in this volume are protected by copyright. Please do not reproduce or perform, whether in part or in whole, excepting for purposes of review, any of the work contained herein without the express, written permission of the author/photographer. Thank you for honoring my Light.

ISBN-13: 978-0-692-94271-0
ISBN-10: 0-692-94271-8

Dedication

To the Divine Light in All. May we come to live, learn, respect, honor and serve one another from that place of purity, seated deep within our very hearts.

This book is a collection of ideas, observations and practices about yoga, devotion and the way of Light. The entries in this volume may serve as a source of self-help for some individuals beginning or already enjoying a physician-approved, hatha-yoga practice. Use of the material in this volume is completely voluntary and can neither replace the assistance of a qualified instructor nor the care and guidance of a competent, licensed medical or mental healthcare practitioner. This book is not a tool for diagnosis. If you have concerns about what is presented here, do not perform, apply or otherwise engage in the principles, ideas or practices contained herein.

Introduction

Yoga's Devotional Light has been in the making for a very long time. The "research" for this book began over twenty years ago, when my husband pulled two hatha-yoga books, in stark black-and-white with spiral bindings, down from our bookshelves, saying, "Here, Julian, these might help you." (I had been overly vocal about a residual sciatic nerve issue from my first and only pregnancy.)

    These first books, from the Himalayan Institute, were not the high-gloss editions which are standard now, but a spare, ascetic's dream version of how-to manuals outlining the process, for a fastidious student, about how to marry movement to the innate Stillness we all carry inside.

With Samskrti, Veda and Judith Franks as models and teachers, I began a solo and introspective approach to my study of yoga's physical postures (asana). What I did not anticipate was how extensive and lasting my relationship with yoga's many facets and Vedic tradition's philosophical schools would become.

During the nascent stages of my entry onto the yogic path, our location did not afford me the luxury of a teacher or group classes. Yet, I never felt I was missing anything, or that I was alone in my practice. Able to travel for a weekend of programming with Pandit T. Rajmani and listening on occasion to tapes by Dr. Usharbudh Arya, I soaked up theory.

Because regular asana practice almost immediately "took the pain away" for the sciatic issue, working with my body—daily and, over the years, for increasing amounts of time—became a joyful, natural habit. Asana practice was an honor performed on behalf of my physical frame, by and for my ready Spirit.

JULIAN LYNN

The commitment to keeping my body balanced via yoga was and is a primary affirmation of life, especially during a later and more significant challenge to my physical health. At the time when I needed the most support, when life's surf seemed to carry me somewhere between worlds, my efforts in yoga redoubled. My asana practice peaked at three hours per day—for two years. Illness taught me to revisit breath regulation (pranayama) and meditation with committed consistency.

I liked living in my "city of 'ten' gates" and was not ready to "kick the frame"— to borrow two expressions from Vedanta. Thus, I turned more fervently to yogic methods to help lengthen my stay. Like many before me, I discovered yoga's ability to function as a life preserver on the high seas of physical impermanence. Yoga may serve to reveal, sustain or mend, as well as offering us clarity of vision or resolution.

For ten years, my hatha yoga practice remained the one reliable space, where I experienced perfect wholeness—an inherent, immutable Stillness. I had touched the Self (Atman). During these hours, I could divest myself of worldly concerns and pick up a package of renewed hope. Whenever my toes flexed to feel the rug's pile beneath my feet, I went *There*, riding the magic carpet to the place from which words turn away.

After two relocations and resurfacing from the most critical phase of my health situation, I finally felt a nudge to join a group class and find an external teacher.

The studio, where I studied, offered classes from six different traditions. A few details in my alignment were adjusted. (One Iyengar-certified instructor informed me that my alignment was exceptional—for a "book" learner.) And, as grateful as I was for the assistance with alignment, I missed my solo practice because, although Atman is immutable, the relationship with Atman is ever unfolding and, in my experience, this relationship is best explored, renewed and maintained in the context of a quiet and private space.

JULIAN LYNN

The dialogue with my internal Universe helped establish my awareness and respect for individual pacing and rhythm, as well as a sense of the sacred in All. In way of full disclosure, contiguous with my dedicated yoga practice was my attendance to a variety of unprogrammed Quaker Meetings, an occasional sit among Buddhist meditation circles—most especially, the Tibetan Buddhists, as well as Sufi healing-circle retreats. And, as a child, I attended a service-oriented and progressive, main-line Protestant Church.

All of these venues and several profound contemplative experiences made contributions toward the strengthening of my relationship with the Divine Thread. Thus, these circumstances, as well as the framing provided by Prem Prakash's translation of Narada's *Bhakti Sutras* (see, *The Yoga of Spiritual Devotion*) were and are the origins of my expanding sensibility and the portal through which I finally approached devotional (bhakti) yoga.

With a more complete sense of the sacred established, my days turned into landscapes of heightened wonder and amazement. I continued testing things in the laboratory of my body while exploring consciousness. Life from this vantage point becomes replete with exquisite details and incredible people, who are working fervently to unfold. An open door to bhakti yoga is one of the greatest gifts hatha yoga is capable of bestowing upon truly dedicated asana practitioners.

As I engaged other methodologies for courting Union within Vedic tradition, my yoga practice expanded further: raja, karma, jnana and mantra. Yet, no matter what I was doing—meditating, serving, studying or, in my case, singing the praises of the Most High—everything continued to coalesce at the bottom of yoga's crucible into a cohesive bhakti practice. Bhakti yoga is the alchemy of creating gold from aligned *Being*.

Ten years after beginning my yoga studies, I went to Canada to certify to

JULIAN LYNN

teach hatha vinyasa yoga. A studio, based in Halifax, Nova Scotia, hosted training through the Buddhist Retreat Center, Dorje Denma Ling. After relocating to the American Southwest, I continued to witness the ability of Vedic tradition's methods and concepts to change lives, among the hundreds of students I served.

Thus, the referential bones of this work rest upon my practice, direct life experiences, years of teaching, as well as the rich resources available through the published works of many other yoga practitioners and authors.

My path would not have been possible if it were not for the printed support of others' works in English (and this list is by no means exhaustive): the two, initial hatha-yoga manuals from the Himalayan Institute, J. Krishnamurti's *Think on These Things*, B.K.S. Iyengar's *Light on Yoga*, Prem Prakash's *The Yoga of Spiritual Devotion*, T.K.V. Desikachar's *The Heart of Yoga*, Shankara's *Crest Jewel of Discrimination*, Patanjali's *Yoga Sutra*,

Paramahansa Yogananda's *Autobiography of a Yogi* (this mention cannot say enough about the role and potency of this work) and Eknath Easwaran's translations of *The Bhagavad Gita* and *The Upanishads*.

In writing *Yoga's Devotional Light*, which is a telescoped compilation of experiences, I wish to provide fellow yoga practitioners with a glimpse into one person's devotional practice. The book is designed neither as a reference work for purists nor is it a how-to manual on bhakti yoga because *the path of devotion is singular and always fully tailored to the individual, her gifts, interests and the exercise of one's own personal freewill.*

Whether or not the narratives included here speak to your current circumstances, I am hopeful they will provide readers with things to consider before finding a sunspot for meditation, stepping onto a yoga mat, singing a spontaneous, made-up song of gratitude or opening a door for a complete stranger. This book is to be written in,

JULIAN LYNN

dog-eared, reread, responded to out loud in the bathtub, quarreled with—or nodded to—and most certainly shared and gifted among studio mates and friends over tea.

    The work's entries fall into three general categories. Short, contemplative pieces act as springboards to daily practice. Medium-length entries might discuss theory or observations about common yogic concepts. (I have chosen to address certain concepts in greater depth than others, while completely omitting certain key items covered thoroughly in other works.) And, in attempting to ground and contextualize the attainments (siddhis), I used a nontraditional and expanded list. Longer essays tell stories about what bhakti yoga looks like in my personal, active daily practice and life.

    As yoga practitioners, we share similar approaches to accessing the Self, and our lives are governed by the same Universal laws (dharma). Yet, the manner in which we are and will be asked to move with the breath and dance with the Divine is as individual, private and sacred in nature as the Universe within ourselves.

Please remember your path is uniquely yours. This book is meant to be a gift. It stands as a record of my path, as it has stood and currently stands, though my relationship with the Self continues to surprise, change, unfold and amaze. Life has taught me to listen, move and respond to the world according to my own nudges.

May the words of encouragement and questions raised here serve to expand the possibilities within you and the Light in your own heart. It is in acknowledging this Light that we come to know the Self and recognize the Self in All.

Julian Lynn
September 2017

The light of Brahman flashes in lightning;
The light of Brahman flashes in our eyes.
It is the power of Brahman that makes
The mind to think, desire, and will. Therefore
Use this power to meditate on Brahman.
He is the inmost Self of everyone...

The Kena Upanishad
Trans. Eknath Easwaran

Winter

1 J. Krishnamurti I

Amid a very late start home after celebrating the holidays one winter, we stop in the cold and the snow of the city to visit the Uptown Used Booksellers. Darkness permeates the ether, and the dim brightness of the streetlights glints off the large, planar stars of a wet, freshly falling snow.

Kicking cakes of snow from my boots, an overwhelming rush of heat greets me as the door's electronic chime sounds when I enter the shop. I am exhausted and not looking forward to the long, dark drive home. Thus, my words to the clerk fall out in abrupt and edgy forms.

"Do you know where I may find a copy of the *I Ching?*"

"You may find it in the New Age section. Or, if it is not there, try the section on Eastern Philosophy. They are next to one another toward the back and to the right," the reply comes.

Browsing through the New Age section, I encounter several translations of *The Chinese Book of Changes*. Pulling several books for consideration, I notice the curious and piquant presence of a middle-aged, Indian man observing me.

"Are you a New Ager?" The question is posed in a lilting, Indian accent and in a semi-comical tone.

Brusque from the perceived intrusion and my own exhaustion, I grumble something to the effect that there is no new age—just a repackaging of traditional Eastern philosophy.

With a hearty chortle, the man exclaims in agreed amusement, "Very old wine, brand new bottle."

My new friend, as it turns out, has just returned from Japan to his local university teaching duties. He talks to me about his experiences of Japanese culture. My preoccupation with my tiredness, the long drive home and my family's waiting all fall away.

"You know, it is not like it is here in the West. The Japanese understand the interconnectedness of all things, of aesthetics and the indestructible nature of energy. They understand the aesthetics of living—of life." The conversation continues.

My friend assures me, "The body may die, but the life force—the energy that drives the body—it is never destroyed. Energy never dies. It may return (my friend's equally loquacious hands gesture, following his words poetically, with the fingertips of one hand tied to his navel and the fingertips of his other hand lifting, tipping and breaking open toward the sky, like a flower head in bloom) to Source."

JULIAN LYNN

This dramatic final gesture snaps me back into real time. With the flower head now opened, I tell my friend that my family is waiting on ice in the car.

"I want you to look for a book, *Think on These Things*, by J. Krishnamurti," he recommends in parting. "It may help you more than the *I Ching*.

I feel a sense of reassurance, on his part, that the book he is recommending will possess, perhaps, answers to some of the questions I have been asking.

2 Teachers

"Advanced" teachers do not bring us into their order or breathing pattern. But, by holding to their singular order and highest Light, they help us realize our own rhythm, order and Self.

YOGA'S DEVOTIONAL LIGHT

3 Stitches

Our thoughts are like stitches we lay down to create a tapestry, in support of the words we express and the actions we take. In turning our thoughts toward service or the care of that which is most precious in ourselves and others, we cannot help but create vibrant speech and rich actions, drawing patterns of connection between our seemingly disparate lives.

4 Inner Peace

Air is the holy vehicle for the Divine elixir and life force, prana. On the inhale, remember this: Breathing is a sacred act.

JULIAN LYNN

5 Story

"Who am I? And, why am I here?" are two traditional questions we are invited to ask ourselves daily as dedicated practitioners of yoga and meditation. Holding ourselves open and steady, we wait for responses from the Self (Atman). This process can prove challenging as the answers may shift daily, depending upon the roles in which we are asked to serve.

Our "I-maker" (ahamkara) may seem fixed with a prepared set of responses pulled from amongst the most ancient nest of stories and narratives we have accepted from others or created about ourselves. If we want to thrive, though, we must be willing to move beyond old injuries and our established script in order to rediscover who we are.

6 A Look Inside

Winter temperatures often shift activities from outside to inside. Each season in nature grants us unique and precious opportunities. At least two, of this chilly season's gifts, are hours for creativity and introspection.

7 Opening

Opening to listen, when we step onto the yoga mat, are seated in meditation or engaged in a contemplative practice, fills the day with heart-centered choices which—when followed by a balanced personality—lead to life-affirming action, positive changes and vital living.

JULIAN LYNN

8 The Frame

Being healthy has so much to do with how we *feel* about living in the body. Our well-being is greatly influenced by the words we select to describe ourselves, our physicality and the frame's unique traits.

Choose to wear a label that celebrates the body's exceptional handcrafted quality, such as, "This garment is one of a kind. Any irregularities in the dye or weave are unique to this item and serve only to enhance its beauty." This awareness allows us to cast aside others' ideas about physical irregularities and sometimes injurious words.

Own your body. It is a sacred, individual and one-of-a-kind garment. Revel in your physical singularity.

9 New

Snow came this morning in thick, wet clumps, christening the ground with an ancient, lace baptismal gown. This day is a new day with incredible possibilities.

10 Body Electric

Grounding in the body often involves something as simple as engaging in a playful, physical activity. When was the last time you laughed?

Run, jump, dance or sing in the most raucous voice possible. Play + laughter = fully grounded joy. (Be mindful of your context, as well as your potential audience; then, cut loose and have fun.)

JULIAN LYNN

11 Bounty

When we feel like we may not have enough, it is frequently the most important time for us to give.

Casting around for several items, once dear and now almost forgotten, collect and give these things away to appreciative friends, an individual in need or a local charitable organization.

With this simple act, emptiness slides away, replaced by a strong, newfound sense of connectedness, lightness, hope and feelings of genuine abundance.

12 Spontaneous

How best to celebrate this day?

13 Changes

Take a chance and consider reinventing yourself. Try a style of behavior, clothing or a manner of speaking previously unexplored. The new person taking notice could be the one person you were meant to meet.

14 Count on It

Calming breath: Inhale for a count of six, hold for a count of two and exhale for a count of eight. Lungs are never overfull and always relaxed. Adjust the ratios and the count to fit your body's comfort level and needs, according to each day's requirements. Explore the breath.

JULIAN LYNN

15 Holy Literature

My friend told me, "The book was almost magnetic."

At the library's media sale, she picked up, then put down and then picked up again the slim and scruffy, small and soft volume of Shankara's *Crest-Jewel of Discrimination*. Its cover is a dull yellow, with Devanagari script atop the boldly transliterated title. The book's natural binding once served as a delicacy for some tiny creatures long since passed. But, it is only *inside* the book that the title is translated into English.

This is how it is with some people. They remain unintelligible jewels, until we look past their external presentation to find the treasures of their inner hearts.

16 J. Krishnamurti II

Winter has long turned the corner on Solstice; the days' walks find me tumbling through greying banks of snow.

Our most singularly notable used bookseller has just moved into a new location. His entire seven-thousand-plus collection of books is in a chaos of boxes, in the shell of a formerly vacant, two-story downtown department store.

Sent on a hunt for *Think on These Things*, the prospects of finding this book amid this chaos are abysmally low. But, I made a promise, and I plan to try.

Approaching the bookseller, I start with the basics, "Do you think you might have a copy of *Think on These Things* by J. Krishnamurti? Would you be able to direct me to the section of the store where it might be?"

JULIAN LYNN

"Try upstairs, between the first and second aisle, about seven to eight rows back," the reply is delivered over a pair of greasy, reading glasses and through a thick and unruly beard.

Taking the stairs slowly, I notice the dust from the bookseller's original location has made the move successfully. (There is a lesson in this.) Boxes are in stacks two to four deep and four to five high. Most boxes are closed. Some boxes are haphazardly torn open by rough movers and, I would imagine, a few additional intrepid book seekers.

Initially, I dutifully count the rows back from the head of the second-floor stairway, until—at the seventh row— I feel a pull, drawing me back to the front of the sixth row. And there, on the very top of an open box about waist height, is an amazingly presentable copy of *Think on*

These Things, just waiting for me to walk it downstairs and buy it.

At the counter, with the book in hand, I pay the seller. Then, I wend my way home carefully over icy sidewalks and through the grey banks of crusty snow, with my nose in my new book recommended by my Indian friend.

17 Simple Living

Twenty-eight hangers live in my closet. If a new, gently used item comes into my care, it is time to let go of another lightly used item I have enjoyed.

Material things are meant to be shared, utilized and actively appreciated. Take a look in your closet right now. Is there anything ready to be passed along and enjoyed by someone in greater need?

JULIAN LYNN

18 Equality

So much work to do yet—for merit to be recognized and valued more than false assumptions or mere physical and external appearances. Live each day from the seat of your merit. Integrity shines.

19 Brightness

Quite often, when we find ourselves in the maze of living our lives as a series of habits, we forget about seeking that which enlivens us or makes us bright. Everyone has something, which when mentioned, makes them glow a little brighter.

For your Self, think about what that something or who that someone is and spend time growing your brightness.

20 Listening

We have been observing silence at home. It is not the cold silence of discontent, but the blossoming silence in celebration of learning how to listen to the subtle pulses of the authentic desires of our individual hearts.

This expanded quiet space pushes us to ask the questions: When do we enjoy the dance with our individual Self? When do we come together to enjoy synergistic communion as a pair? And, finally, when will we accept the invitation to take a turn and dance with the ultimate and infinite Partner?

What a gift to be given the space, freedom and quiet time to listen and grow from the inside out.

JULIAN LYNN

21 Changing Habits

Stripping ourselves of old, inefficient habits and outmoded responses renders the mundane poetic and the stale refreshed. Look up! The sky will appear clearer, deeper in color. And, moving through the scheduled course of a day will begin to feel lighter. Breathe anew.

22 Neighbors

I awoke to a freshly shoveled walk this morning. What a surprise. Thank you, dear friends! Life Rule#1: Kindness begets kindness. Come to know your neighbors through kindnesses, and they may become your most cherished and reliable allies.

23 Cleansing

    Rewriting life scenes is one method of working through that which remains unresolved in the heart. Coming to center, recall a situation in which you or someone you know behaved in a manner that was less than optimal for all hearts involved. Reenvision that circumstance in a way that your heart enters into a state of quiet peace, finding Stillness.

    If emotions other than compassion, new understanding or forgiveness arise, the ego is engaged. To remain in the heart and release painful, unwanted emotions, use a regulated breathing pattern (pranayama); and, return to this practice, until a state of internal and uninterrupted peace is achieved.

JULIAN LYNN

24 Vibrant

Sometimes, after completing a practice, we have glimpses of a brighter world, where colors are more vibrant, flavors more piquant and sounds seem purer in tone than ever before. It is not the world that has changed, but our perceptions of the world have changed.

Through our personal practice, we are able to peel away layers of inaccurate perception or understanding (avidya) to reveal all that is truly luminescent.

25 Five Words

Unlimited Love is all around.

26 Sacred Care

Walking, while cogitating on some old stuff, I had worked myself into quite a fierce, growly state. I was completely in my own head. The perfect sky, the natural beauty of my context and the peace of an almost empty street went unnoticed, as I walked along.

Then, a car pulled up to the four-way stop directly in front of me at the corner, where I was about to cross. We were alone, the car and I.

The driver's-side, tinted window rolled smoothly down to the door frame, and a favorite yoga student turned to me to say, "I do hope you are having a good day. Namaste." With that, she gave me a respectful nod and drove off.

Then, the black clouds of my own creation began to shift, breaking apart.

JULIAN LYNN

The sun made its way into my thoughts. And, I realized again how important it is for us to be here for one another—to *free* each other from the storm clouds of our own creation—with a few thoughtful and kind words. This is sacred care.

27 Without Words

Vedic tradition is rich in vocabulary, describing a wide range of spiritual states. Yet, when we find the Sanskrit word we want to describe our experience, there are often four, five or six English words that are not quite equivalent—but close—to what we have experienced.

This is when it is best to remain quiet and in gratitude for our amazing and much changed state. Why try and label everything? Live in the Mystery.

28 Point of Entry

In Stillness, there is an opportunity to live in a larger sphere. Concerns shift, from personal comforts and wants, toward the needs and necessities of others. The scope of our worldview widens as we begin seeing the manner in which our gifts might aid more people—or one person—more completely. This awareness is the entry onto the path.

29 Gold Coins

For one day, work on the assumption that words are as weighty as genuine, gold coins. Choose and share them sparingly. Spend wisely.

JULIAN LYNN

30 Tattoos

"Is that a permanent tattoo I see on your leg?" I approach one of my newer yoga students. She is lying flat on her back with her legs straight up the wall. Her pant legs are hovering just below her inverted thighs, "above" the knee.

"Yes, it was my birthday gift to myself when I turned seventy. I am thinking about getting another tattoo for my seventy-fifth birthday," she reflects.

Then, the class becomes involved.

"What is it?" another student pipes up. Voices float and drift as if from the very floor. Everyone is in the same inversion.

"It is a pattern—beautiful and fully pigmented—in the shape of an elongated oval," I report, then cue, "Pull your toes toward your knees. Push through your heels. Enjoy the stretch on the backs of the calves. Have some fun with this. Alternate pushing through your heels, with pointing and extending your toes. Then, alternate what your feet are doing as well—one foot pushes through the heel while the other foot extends with toes."

"Mmmmm. This feels good. Just what I needed," another student hums, and then asks the first student, "What possessed you to get a tattoo?"

"It's *my* body. I wanted to celebrate turning seventy. My conservative children think it's awful—that *I* am awful—'a terrible influence on my grandchildren,' they say. In fact, I have to keep it covered when I go to visit my daughter, which is difficult in southern, sunny Texas with a beach and pool. I would do it again though." Her mischievous smile breaks through everything, adding to the delivery of her response.

I take the break in the conversation

JULIAN LYNN

to remind everyone, "Coming back to center, exhale for a count of seven. Inhale for a count of seven, then hold the lungs comfortably full for one count—minding your lung capacity and the cadence of your own breathing rhythm."

Then, to myself, I think, "Is that not what we all want to do—to become owners and celebrators of our bodies?"

31 By the Numbers

The average number of respirations per day for a man is 26,100 (a woman may take up to 29,000 breaths per day).

Slow things down and even things out to establish an internal sense of equilibrium and tranquility. It may lead to calmer days and extended contentment.

32 Ease

Stillness may be experienced more freely in meditation than almost any other circumstance, and it comes with greater frequency and ease through the regular practice of breath regulation.

Pranayama is a sumptuous anteroom, leading into the many-roomed mansion of the sanctified heart. Enter. Passage into the hall of Light will be granted.

33 Goodness

Let us be good to one another for as long as we are together. Life is a gift.

JULIAN LYNN

34 Tender Shoot

Stepping onto the path of self-discovery requires a close circle of supportive friends, working as carefully and pointedly—as we are—on making thoughtful life choices. Sometimes old friendships and acquaintances give way to make room for new, more supportive and encouraging faces.

Do not mourn excessively over the loss of these older relationships. But, in the context of devotional practice, celebrate, thank and bless each kind and troubled heart, who has ever helped you learn more about yourself or another human being.

Each relationship is a momentary gift, as we journey along our way, and a blessing of potential learning.

35 Patterns

Finding ourselves falling into long-worn patterns that are no longer comfortable, we push away from them within the sanctuary of our physical practice and during the context of our dedicated meditations. Reservoirs of strength and creative solutions are revealed in these contexts, so that we may reimagine, rewrite and find a new balance in the calendar of our days.

36 Separateness

Getting lost in issues of identity or individuality, we lose sight of how we are joined in life. Reach for a friendly hand.

JULIAN LYNN

37 Glamour

So much of what I do, as an aspirant on the path of devotion, is without a trace of external charm or elegance. There is often nothing socially enchanting about ways in which I am asked to serve.

Walking my path, in alignment with clear guidance through meditation, renders me almost invisible or, at least, quite often externally and socially insignificant—whether I am opening a door for an elderly man, sharing a pop-top canned good with a homeless person, taking garden produce to a neighbor or picking up litter while dog walking.

The expression of devotion may or may not include a life of social glamour. To date, there has been no high-end yoga fashion, no svelte, hardbody photo shoot nor magazine cover. Yet, elegance, charm and enchantment are more than amply supplied by the sweet and heightened relationship with All that is most surely of and from the Divine hand.

38 Into the Heavens

Yoga peels layers away from the pit in the fruit of our Being. That pit, hard and crusty as it is, guards and protects the seed of an entire, internal Universe—until we are ready to open and fling ourselves into the stars and the heavens.

Nurture the Self while journeying; nourish the body with pure water, sunlight, healthy foods, holy friends and laughter. Your Universe is ready to spin.

JULIAN LYNN

39 Bodies

    Bodies are designed to move. The noise of modern living makes following the body's subtle cues challenging.

    Fresh air opens communications throughout the frame. Breathe deeply! In following the cadence of the breath, learn to trust again, and begin to listen to the purified body's true will.

40 Cravings

Winter sunlight plays across the neighbor's wooden fence. The black walnut tree's long, craggy arms bob in the wind, in shadowy relief, craving Union with the spare, chill sky.

41 Life's Sweetness

Upon concluding my presentation, a woman confessed to me that she felt guilty for having enjoyed a sweet, after-lunch treat, commenting that she felt she had made a "bad" choice.

"Why would the Divine not want you to taste life's sweetness?" I asked her. "Life is full of possibilities, sensations, sounds, colors and flavors. Sweetness is but one of them. If we are able to savor and enjoy what is before us, without harm to ourselves or others, why wouldn't the Divine approve?

"We delight the Divine when we are able to embrace living and relish life's pleasures—most especially, when we are compelled to share them with others."

JULIAN LYNN

42 Bhakti Yoga

The practice of yoga is so much more than the physical activity we engage in a few times a week on a sticky mat. Any choices we make that create in us feelings of reverence, gratitude for life's details, a subtle sense of communion with our own *Being* or the precious rhythm of another's or fellow creature's existence should be recognized as yoga's genuine practice.

This is living devotional yoga.

43 Reset

While camping, I awoke to light flurries and a pale, grey winter sky. One full week of camping resets the body—ready to go! Earthing is...the best.

44 The End of Gossip

"What is up with that? The breaks and all?" intones one of my coworkers.

"I don't know. But, I think he has a drug problem. Have you ever noticed how glassy his eyes are? They seem to be worse after break," I offer my observations.

"I wouldn't care if we all had breaks."

"And full lunches," I add.

Most of us at work are in our early twenties and going somewhere—graduate school, overseas or onto better jobs. The team we create in our fast-paced, work environment is efficient, professional and fun, perhaps because we know that this job is not forever. Every client would like his order to be have been completed yesterday or, at the very least, immediately, but the sheer volume of orders does not allow it. Thus, it is no

JULIAN LYNN

surprise that breaks are almost impossible. Trips on the elevator to the fourth floor are allowed only on a per-need basis. Lunches are half-eaten sandwiches, munched between orders and with hands hastily wiped on work smocks.

    The perception of the crew is that there is only one fly in the ointment of our efficiently-running team, a thirty-four-year-old man who has somehow escaped promotion into management and who is perceived as *other* by the rest of us. There is discussion, conjecture and, sometimes, gossip about our older teammate, Gary.

    Gary is an oddity in many respects. His hair is meticulously coiffed in a throwback style, secured with hair spray. (Who wears hair spray anymore?) Gary does not fly around the shop but moves with a precise stiffness that makes him look like an automaton, which is what we

YOGA'S DEVOTIONAL LIGHT

are in this machine of a place, but would rather not believe ourselves to be.

    The trait, causing the greatest amount of rancor and the source of the most vicious talk, is that Gary is allowed to observe both of his fifteen-minute breaks and a full, half-hour lunch. His breaks are all out-of-store. He and the manager have a code of nods they use in signaling when it is okay for Gary to take his leave from the store and the team.

    "I am going to ask him what is up with the breaks and stuff," I announce to my coworker and friend.

    "Only you would," she responds in short and quite truthfully.

    "I am tired of talking about it. I will find out what is going on when we work together on evenings and alone."

    "Go for it, and tell me what you find out," she responds.

JULIAN LYNN

It takes over a week before I am assigned to work an evening shift alone with Gary. And, before I can ask any questions, we have to be caught up with orders, and there must be a lull in traffic. Then, a window of opportunity appears.

"So, Gary, there is a lot of chat around the store about your getting to take all of your breaks and coming back glassy-eyed. What more are you doing up on the fourth floor with your break time?"

After a considerably long pause and some paper shuffling, Gary begins speaking. "Well, I *am* doing something *more* on the fourth floor during my breaks. That is when I take my pain medication. I have rheumatoid arthritis. I take painkillers by injection to be able to get through my work days."

Into the space of my stunned silence, Gary proceeds with a long train of stories about his life and circumstances. I listen,

YOGA'S DEVOTIONAL LIGHT

feeling wretchedly inadequate as a human being and fully unworthy of receiving the scope of stories this man is willingly sharing with me.

Finally, as I move into some sort of contorted self-forgiveness for my brash insensitivity, I venture forth with another, different question distilled from the narrative Gary has offered.

"You are a trivia buff on 1970's rock music?" I ask in amazement.

"Yes, ask me any question you like. I can give you the full discography on most everything. Name it."

Mentally flipping through my own limited, internal database of 1970's rock music, I venture forward with something obscure, "Hmmm, the song, 'Go All the Way'—who sang it?"

"The Raspberries released that song in July of 1972. Want to try another?" Gary is beaming with success.

JULIAN LYNN

"This is amazing. And, it explains your hair," the internal realization escapes from my oh-so-open mouth.

Unoffended at being recognized, Gary's grin stretches in broad gratitude across his face. The rest of our unusually slow shift passes with easy, jocular conversation about 1970's music and one-hit wonders.

A few days later, while working with my closest work friend, she queries me, "What did you find out about Gary?"

"He has a medical condition. If you want to know more, you will have to ask him. No more conjecture or gossip."

Life Lesson: The gossip of conjecture injures, never informing us about another person's circumstances—ever.

45 Patterns

Devotion is an action verb in disguise.

YOGA'S DEVOTIONAL LIGHT

46 Forecast

Another brilliantly cold and blustery day yawns. The sun hangs blazing and luminescent in the sky.

The sun is a reminder to remain luminescent within the context of the Self; so, that no matter what the external forecast, our internal forecast remains a constant state of sunshine.

47 Nourishing

In Eastern healing modalities, the respiratory system is often considered the body's first means of nourishment and digestion. Breathe with the intention of *feeding* your whole body.

JULIAN LYNN

48 Traveling

One function of the traditional yogic behavioral observances (yama and niyama), from Patanjali's *Yoga Sutra*, is to act as a system of checks and balances as our dialogue with the Self develops. (Are my intentions and actions truly non-harming? Am I engaging in activities that are an appropriate use of my sacred and vital personal energy?)

Actions must become Self-supportive, as well as honoring the long-term health and vitality of the community around us. Once, we are established in our methods of traveling our spiritual path, we become free to assist others, without injuring anyone, according to our abilities and others' stated needs.

49 Sensations

Touch is often the sense we are least aware of because it is the sense we use the most frequently and automatically.

Come fully into the body today and notice the hot, cold, soft and hard details that touch you. How does life feel?

50 Reading

Early in life, we are taught to override our raw, emotional impressions; yet, our first, unedited emotional impressions may provide critical keys to our coming to know the longings of the unheeded Spirit.

Reading is a skill. Learning to read our emotions is one door to the Self. This skill may be taught, learned, honed and, ultimately, mastered.

JULIAN LYNN

51 Non-harming

Employing the principle of non-harming (ahimsa), we are invited to engage with the world in a more peaceful manner—without wittingly doing harm to ourselves or others.

More than anything, non-harming involves shifting from ego-based social engagement to service-oriented social engagement, with a tender eye toward self-care and a critical look at how we behave as consumers.

When we shift from asking, "What's in it for me?" to asking, "How may I serve the greater good in this context?"—we will have begun the process of removing the root obstacles that cause pain and damage to our most sacred Self and that which is most holy in All beings.

52 Eye Candy

Third-eye activity is called, by some, distracting, eye candy. In truth, visual, third-eye activity stands as a helpful marker for distinct meditative states. If you experience visible, third-eye activity be in gratitude for the additional tool of awareness in your meditative practice.

53 Fog

Waking near the lake, a dense fog renders the immense body of water invisible. A few steps and the lake reveals itself. How often are we separated from Reality in this way, with our knowing clouded by the fog of misperception?

JULIAN LYNN

54 Truth

As occidental thinkers, we are inclined to envision the yogic observation of truth (satya) as something inviting externalization through speech, judgment or argumentation, defending that which we perceive to be right or just. The practice of truth may actually involve bearing silent witness to our own manner of Being in the world or reviewing our behavior in a variety of relationships.

The process of witnessing our personal truth, in this manner, aids us in becoming more thoughtfully skilled in how we place our vital energy, rendering our thoughts, words and actions consistent reflections of the most pure intentions and desires held in the very depths of our hearts.

55 The Sun Inside

Warm, cold, sunny, rainy—nonetheless, it is from the weather inside of ourselves that we respond to those sentient beings around us.

What is today's internal weather like? Are things calm, comfortable and light?

56 High Winds

Combing through the trees to release old, dry branches, the breath of the very Earth herself makes way for renewed growth. Trails of dead twigs are ready to be collected as we prepare to celebrate a change in seasons.

Winter shall pass. We are waiting for you, Spring!

JULIAN LYNN

57 Non-stealing

Non-stealing (asteya) is sometimes considered the not-even-forgetting-to-leave-work-pens-at-work observance for yoga practitioners. This application of the observance includes this notion, as well as including the idea—when non-stealing is properly embedded into everyday consciousness—that we are being prepared to receive from the Divine hand that which we most require while releasing the desire to accumulate more than we need.

Thus, non-stealing is much more than avoiding the taking of objects that are not ours. Non-stealing, in the broadest sense, may also imply the processes of giving away freely, that which we do not require. Giving freely allows us to receive freely, and with gratitude, what we truly need.

58 Release

Tension loses its grip when the mind grows calm. The mind grows calm walking through the door leading into the grand hall of meditation. Step over the threshold. All are welcome.

59 Soil

My fingers still show traces from the moist, rich earth in our garden beds.

What a privilege to be able to grant a homestay to some of my fellow, green inhabitants here on earth. These plants most certainly appreciate being able to stretch their "toes" in the ground, just as I enjoy stretching my toes in the context of my physical practice.

JULIAN LYNN

60 Vital Energy

When actively engaged in the appropriate use or application of our personal, vital energy (brahmac[h]arya), we experience the uniqueness of our discrete Self functioning seamlessly within the context of a healthy, social whole, if the whole is also life-respecting and respectful of Universal principles.

When in alignment with this observance, regular practitioners describe feelings of heightened completeness, as if they are gliding through activities and duties on the physical realm—with assistance. Doors open, synchronicities occur and timely support is both granted and extended. The world begins to feel like a place of supreme, Divine order.

61 Around the Edges

For my busiest students and clients, the most convenient way to create three, five-minute sessions for daily breathwork is by selecting a safe place to park (before work, during lunch and after errands) to tuck in an in-vehicle practice. If at all possible, find a green space to park, lock your doors and simply BREATHE.

62 Rain

The rains have come. The dry earth and her plants loosen their hold on a tight and gripping existence. Toes wiggle. Feet shift. Palms open and arms rise. The sun speaks through the clouds to touch all who reach up in humble gratitude. Salutations.

JULIAN LYNN

63 Non-possessiveness

Even more than offering us a guideline on our relationships with physical objects or phenomena, non-possessiveness (aparigraha) reminds us to detach ourselves from the "I, me and mine" to dedicate all that we have and do to the "we, us and our"—the greater whole.

Thus, non-possessiveness supports the concept of selfless service. By working to alleviate suffering and discomfort through the redistribution of goods, we are ultimately liberated to walk more freely in aid of others. This is the way in which we come to hold more nonphysical and emotionally true luxury and wealth, in the form of authentic personal connections, than we could ever have imagined or otherwise dreamed of possessing.

64 A Mantle of Grace

Opening the day with meditation, I make an inquiry about how best to step forth into community. A walk to the coffee house seems to be in order.

Peeling my knapsack off, once I have arrived, I set my things down on the couch at the window. Today's crowd is a loosely acquainted crew of familiar faces.

To my left is the grandmother from Ireland, whose ankle tattoo announces her love and longing for the Emerald Isle. The barista is only obvious as her head bobs because of her behind-the-counter activities. There are two, solo college students with lean, swinging legs draped over cafe stools at the tall tables in back.

After more than three hours of online work, brain fog sets in. Grabbing my handbag, I take a bathroom break.

JULIAN LYNN

Drawing my mind together to shine a light through the internal numbness, I open to ask my Self, "Where next?"

Preoccupied with my thoughts, I head back to the couch to collect my sundries. A draft of bitterly cold air rounds the main door to snap at me as I unplug my computer. A homeless woman has come in to catch some heat and use the facilities. *This is a place of humanity.*

Still absent-mindedly wondering what I am up to next, I bus my dishes, walking them to the end of the counter.

Emerging from the back hall, the homeless woman is carrying my purse high in her hand. I can see her red, chafed knuckles. She asks in an overly loud voice, "Does this belong to anyone?"

I raise my hand to meet hers, "Yes, that would be mine. Thank you!" And, before I can offer her any concrete act of gratitude, she is gone out into the cold.

YOGA'S DEVOTIONAL LIGHT

Heads are shaking and tongues cluck, "You had better check to make sure everything is in there. You are lucky."

"Everything is here—nothing missing," the report goes out. Inside of my Self, I sense the integrity of character and blessed trait of non-attachment the homeless woman carries in her heart.

Silently, I wish her a safe journey for this day and every day. May she be protected by the Divine hand and a mantle of endless Grace.

65 Vows

Practice yoga every day? Holy Union is best left unbroken. Choose karma, jnana, bhakti, raja, hatha or mantra yoga to fill every space within your day, and renew your vows with your highest Light.

JULIAN LYNN

66 Why Wait?

Last night, I slept on the floor with my older dog. She was recovering from a dental cleaning. Dogs must be sedated for this procedure. Thus, a dental cleaning for a dog is major surgery. Postoperatively, her teeth looked great, but she was barely embodied. I kept thinking, "Why did we wait so long, when it was obviously necessary and the right thing to do?" (As a side note, her joint health improved notably within two weeks of the cleaning.)

Why do any of us put off the care we need? It is time to take that walk, eat that incredible plate of fresh fruit or laugh heartily over a funny movie.

Signed,
The Tooth Faerie

P.S. Don't forget to floss.

67 Family Life

In the intimacy and demand of family life, we sometimes forget that there is a completeness inside of us, as individuals, reaching for our full potential. This is the Self, asking to be honored. Set time aside each day to listen to that One voice.

68 Body Machine

Please sit or stand. Raise all ten toes, while flexing both hands and lifting and opening the chest. Exhale out everything that is stale. Inhale the very breath of life, announcing to yourself, "Beautiful, poetic body machine. You are perfect, and I am grateful for you."

69 Hot Yoga

Being from a hatha-yoga tradition that encourages the building of heat (tapas) from the inside out, purification by heat comes naturally as a result of actively using the appropriate breathing practices in conjunction with optimal sequencing of the most appropriate postures.

Nonetheless, many of us feel drawn to hot yoga for what it does to our bodies after class. (Hot yoga was first championed in the West to replicate the weather conditions of southern India.)

There is something utterly exhausting and deliciously decadent about the melt-you-to-your-bones heat. Check with your physician to determine what is right for you. And, then, if it is appropriate, sample with extreme care.

70 Order

Faith, as a concept, shifts from the abstract to the concrete with a simple step into the sphere of Nature.

Take a walk outside. Open your eyes. The world is indeed wide.

71 Checking In

Do I have fresh air?
Do I have access to clean water?
Do I have healthy foods to eat?
Do I have safe shelter?

If we can answer all of these questions in the affirmative, we must move into a state of simple gratitude.

72 Peace Returns

How has your day been? So far, so good, sunshine?

Frayed emotions, frazzled nerves and scattered energy have the opportunity to transform themselves into a freshly pressed linen cloth or a smoothly operating machine through a simple shift into one of the regulated breathing practices from pranayama.

Exhale out all that is not of your highest Light. Then, inhale sunlight to a count of seven, collecting all that is of your pure essence into and around your body. Again, exhale to a count of seven, and inhale to seven, repeating this pattern, until your breathing is even and peace returns to you.

73 Choices

    Sunlight streams in, through late-winter's window pane, hot and insistent. The heat feels good. Outside, the cool air calls to be warmed in my body, on a brisk and lengthy walk.

    There is a full-scale tug of war going on inside of me. Go outside or stay inside? Ample personal choices, such as these, are a luxury beyond measure.

74 Shedding

    The debris of the past scatters into the wind as senses are attuned to the heart. In Stillness, external chatter falls away — a carapace never meant to be worn.

JULIAN LYNN

75 Who Are You?

  A man in his mid-twenties comes to our door asking to use the phone. My husband takes the inquiry because I am out on a walk with the dogs.

  Approaching our tiny covered porch, I observe a clean-shaven man with very closely cropped hair, seated on our only piece of porch furniture, a backless, rescued chair. He is lean—the type of lean that makes the trained sculptor in me want to fill in the cave of his belly and build-out the sinewy musculature of his body with extra clay, while the mom in me wants to feed him. His frame is functioning as a hanger for his short-sleeved t-shirt and loose jeans, not as any kind of protection from the unforgiving, biting winds today.

I sidle past the scene with the dogs in tow in mild consternation. Mine has been a long walk on a brutally damp and cold day. The man in our 'chair' sits doubled over with one forearm across his midriff to conserve what heat his body is generating, while shakily punching numbers into a phone with his free hand. Stepping inside the house to give the man some privacy, my husband follows me and the dogs inside. Behind the front door, I unzip my winter jacket hanging it on the coat rack.

"He is freezing," I comment tersely on the obvious. "I would give him the ski jacket I am wearing, but I don't think pink and white are his colors."

Gazing at the coat rack, my husband states philosophically, "I don't know what his deal is, but he certainly isn't dressed for this weather."

"What jacket do you have that we can spare?" I ask.

JULIAN LYNN

"I am thinking about that now."

"You've been back from burying your father for six months now and have not worn that new jean jacket once. It is clean, the sleeves are long enough for his frame, and the weave is tight enough to offer some protection from this wind. I cannot think of a more appropriate jacket to donate," I offer.

"Yes, I agree," my husband responds. "He needs it more than I do."

Hearing the timbre of the man's voice break off, we step outside with the jean jacket in hand.

"Did you reach the person you were trying to call?" my husband asks politely.

"I suppose, though I don't think it solved anything." His answer is quiet, and he is downcast, defeated.

"I hope that everything works out for you," my husband counters attempting to speak optimistically.

YOGA'S DEVOTIONAL LIGHT

"Yeah, me too," the man responds, handing back the phone.

Handing the man the jean jacket, my husband says, "It looks like you might need this today. It's an extra you can have."

Rising from his seated position, with his voice expressing curious wonder, the man asks, "*Who are you people?* Are you Christians or hippies?"

76 celestial

Each healing modality has a core philosophical notion behind it. In Ayurveda, it is the idea that each of us is our own unique and complete Universe.

Respect your whole celestial being. Begin to look upon those around you with the same polite, consideration. And, it will feel like Heaven is unfolding.

JULIAN LYNN

77 Remembering

In Vedic tradition, the baby in the womb says, "I will remember. I will remember...that I possess a Divine spark, what I have learned from previous incarnations and how to love and be loved." With birth, it seems all is forgotten. We approach our mats and meditation cushions to take our requests of remembrance to the Supreme Self.

78 Refinement

Slipping into the moment, with the whole of our singular, conscious Being is akin to putting on the perfect garment for a preordained party. Be present for the Party. You were most certainly invited.

79 Transitions

There comes a point, whether we are on our yoga mats, practicing breath regulation or committed to our daily meditations, when our internal dialogue shifts. What was once "I need...", "I want..." or "I should..." becomes "What do I truly need?", "What do I really want?" and "What is the best use of my time?" The transition, to asking these new, internal questions, is pivotal and, if we choose to listen, potentially transformative.

Stay open to the nudges and clues that come in, following through with wise, appropriate responses. Honor your yogic commitment to nonharmful behavior both toward your Self and that of Self in others whom you meet.

JULIAN LYNN

Spring

80 Better

While growing up, my family did not own a truck. And, as an avid gardener, there were times when my father needed to borrow a friend's pickup to haul large loads of fertilizer, compost or woodchips.

Each time we finished using another person's vehicle, all of us participated in washing the truck and, then, went to fill the tank with fuel. I asked my father why we went to the trouble of washing an already dirty truck and, not only replacing the gasoline we had used, but filling the tank completely.

True to form, my father's answer was thoughtful, terse and straightforward, "Always leave things in a better condition than you find them."

JULIAN LYNN

81 Garden Party

As I churned the leaves into the earth yesterday, the worms and I had our own tea party in the garden. The sun was sweet in contrast to the cool air.

Oh, what a wonder it would be to find the right words for the joy that fills all creatures at the celebratory breakup of winter's last hold on the Earth!

82 Hugs

Rolling yourself into a ball, with the spine resting on a comfortably padded floor, gather folded knees to the chin. Wrap your arms across both shins. Rock yourself gently. Delight will set in.

83 Purity

Purity (s[h]auc[h]a), the first of the internal observations, may sound like an impossibility, but this recommendation invites us to attend to the cleanliness, both internal and external, of our physical vehicle, as well as considering the nature of the *motivations* behind our actions.

In cultivating an expanding awareness around purity, we are asked to attend to the deepest parts of our internal, unseen world—our core intentions. After caring tenderly and appropriately for our individual body and highest Light, we must ask this question: Am I functioning from a pure, unattached heart, while attempting to attend to the physical, emotional, intellectual or spiritual needs of my Self and the Self in those around me?

JULIAN LYNN

84 Dreaming

Dreamless sleep is considered one of the most restorative states of being in yogic tradition. But, what of dream-filled sleep? Some would say that this is a state of being when our psyches engage in some very deep and potentially efficient psychological housekeeping. Perhaps the most important thing to remember is that we must remain open to what the heart is trying to say through the cinematic window of the "resting" mind.

85 Acorn

Score the seed; plant and nurture your Atman in the very best soil, because The Tree of Life is inside of you.

86 Contentment

Contentment (samtos[h]a) with life usually involves reflecting on the small gifts and comforts granted to us daily, wherever those gifts and comforts may be found. Feelings of contentment also flow most easily when we cultivate gratitude for the variety of experiences we initiate, encounter or participate in, through the volition of others.

Stop to consider that a clean glass of fresh, potable water is indeed a miracle. Over time, as gratitude grows so does our sense of overwhelming personal contentment. The heart will come to brimming in a desire to share the most basic of life's needs with those who are currently living without.

JULIAN LYNN

87 Pure Heart

In the context of a pure, unified heart, there is no public/private split or difference in presentation of one's overall personality—only compassion for the fragmented and broken-hearted.

88 Spiritual Reality

There is a physical appearance to scenes, objects and people; and, then, there is the spiritual Reality.

Do not rely on physical presentation to make your most important decisions. Find the Stillness inside, and your calm, centered heart will help you discern your current, working truth. This awareness will guide you on your path—forward, around or through.

89 Purification

For practitioners of hatha yoga, purification (tapas) or practice causing change—literally "heat"—takes us to our mats. In the context of asana practice, we create the space needed to attend to the deeper work of revealing the blocks remaining unexplored in the recesses of our minds, bodily tissues and hearts.

"Heat" helps us cleanse and realign. The blocks we come up against are not only physical, but also ethical and emotional impurities we must release before we can move forward.

Regular practice exposes us to the known and unknown issues needing to be addressed on the path toward optimal thought, speech and action. This is how we come to know who we really are.

JULIAN LYNN

90 Tending

Students sometimes express concern that they may never have an experience of yogic Union or Samadhi. And, yet, most everyone who has ever tended a campfire knows what it is like to forget about time, have no concept of location and feel her personal edges fall away.

Yogic Union is a matter of tending one's internal, infinite Flame with the same degree of intensity.

91 Hitch a Ride

Spontaneous joy, nabbed at a city park on the swings, a skateboard or a slide, is fun for all ages and at all times.

92 self-study

Cartographers speak about a cat's-eye view versus an eagle's-eye view of a given landscape. In many ways, self-study (svadhyaya) demands the same shift in us, movement from surface to air.

Once aloft, the process of observing ourselves in habituated patterns is often humbling. Therefore, it is important that we have first grown skilled in our abilities to forgive, extend compassion and love others because we will need to extend these same qualities and emotional attitudes toward ourselves.

Compassionate self-study teaches us how to cultivate and mark our very personal and tender growth. Be gentle with yourself. You are growing.

JULIAN LYNN

93 Focus

Our perceptions or created narratives about other people and their lives are often incomplete and quite inaccurate. Rather than placing effort into imagining another person's life or circumstances, why not place effort into creating or reworking your own? This is the more appropriate placement of sacred, vital energy.

94 Expressive Filters

Photographic filters exist so that a camera's record of our visual experiences — of a place, person or still life — relates how we *feel* about what went on, while we were fully present to that moment.

95 Surrender

Perhaps the most delicately sumptuous of observances is the notion of surrender (is[h]varapranidhana), which is often translated as surrender to a Higher Power. This concept is not about dominance or subservience, as the English translation would imply, but it is about being called or beckoned to dance—while respecting the sanctity of our personal rhythm—with the sacred flow of unified Life.

When in this mode, we revel in the unique gifts, roles and relationships, granted to us as the timeline of our life unfolds on a moment by moment basis. These gifts, roles and relationships become observable blessings. Life becomes an observable, moving parade of wonder.

JULIAN LYNN

96 Bicycles

On my bicycle, en route to the coffee house, I see a man standing astraddle his bicycle in a large parking lot bent over a slip of paper. His forearms are resting on his handlebars. Because of the mode of transportation we are both using, I know we are part of the same informal family of cyclists. Doubling back to determine whether or not I can be of assistance, I cut the edge of the parking lot with the precision of a knife freeing a warm cake from its pan. Braking in front of my unknown friend, I ask him whether or not he needs any help.

"I am supposed to be at this address within one-half hour. But I can't find it. Do you know where this street is?"

"I am still fairly new to town, but I know the city is set up on a grid. I will show you where one of the two cross streets is. I think the railroad tracks might have confused things. We can find out together whether or not you need to be north or south of the tracks."

"Do you have time?" he asks, his face is still pinched in worry about the time.

This question trips me up on an old, frayed cord that I have been working to release during my spiritual practice. Not having "enough time" for another human being or fellow creature is keyed into notions of inflated self-importance and a certain social conceit (i.e. my time is worth more than your time) effectively blocking the path to the most sacred heart.

"Yes, I have time to help," I affirm. "I will start out, and you can follow me."

"I will be right behind you." The sense of relief in his voice is palpable.

Circling around, we head in the opposite direction from the way in

JULIAN LYNN

which he had been bicycling. We are returning to the west side of town. At the street separating the east from the west side of town, I stop my bicycle to show him how to read the street signs for address and directional indicators.

"I know the streets over here are less regular because of the railroad tracks," I shout into the wind, hoping that my words are being carried back to my new bicycling companion.

Stopping near the address he was hoping to find, we are greeted by the signage of a local mission house for jobless and homeless people.

As he pulls his bicycle next to my own, I observe, "This is sort of an odd street—the way it is angled. I'm glad we found the address you needed." I nod my head in the direction of the low building with people all around.

YOGA'S DEVOTIONAL LIGHT

Hanging his head apologetically, he explains, "I lost my job recently. I had been staying with relatives, but they can't house me unless I can pay rent. I am homeless now. Do you need any money? I have some money. I can pay you for guiding me here."

"No, but thank you for offering. You keep that money for yourself. I am so sorry to hear about your current circumstances. You can do me one favor though—instead of thinking, 'I am homeless now,' try thinking, 'I will have a place to call home very soon.' This is the image that I will hold in my mind for you. Okay? Best wishes!"

Pushing off from the gravel with my right foot, we nod to one another in acknowledgement. In reality, I am the one who has most been served and honored today during this encounter.

JULIAN LYNN

Three blocks later, I must stop my bike to collect myself and take a moment to sit in gratitude for the gift of spiritual service I have received, by guiding my new friend to a safer place. I wish we could all find places of safety to call home.

97 Faith

Revisiting our matrix of beliefs which comprise our faith (s[h]raddha), we may look into the space of our consciousness to find a grab bag of ideas keeping us from our true Perfection.

Dump out the grab bag of crusty notions. Shed the old, worn-out, scarred and scaly skin. Take your new and tender form to a safe place, and bask under the sun of renewal.

98 Bandhas

The bandhas are a system of "locks" used in asana practice to help regulate the flow of energy within the body.

Sanskrit, as an Indo-European language, shares many phonemes with the English language. The word in English that is related to bandhas is bondage.

The bandhas are like the locks present on a canal connecting two waterways. Appropriate use of the root, pelvic, jaw and tongue locks allows even the newest of students to open doors to certain states. Find a qualified instructor to learn about the bandhas. Expand your practice.

99 Consolidation

What is your breath saying?

JULIAN LYNN

100 Water

Rain, humidity, puddle boots and everything is reminding me of water — the water within, between and without. Flow with it. Share it. Pour it. Quench your thirst. Move into it.

Sometimes on the mat, I like to envision moving with the postures through water. The image provides both resistance and lift. Like any committed relationship, hatha yoga assists us with the process of revealing who we are, by causing us to bump up against what we perceive ourselves to be in relationship to others.

Pass through the mirage of self-importance. Choose to be extra thoughtful and generous, while treading gently in the communal pool.

101 Burst

The living aesthetic, then, for a regular practitioner of sense withdrawal (pratyahara) is very different from that of one unschooled in the practice.

One flower bud provides as much or more joy than an entire bouquet of fully extended blossoms. Potential or future sensory pleasure is delivered in current time from a single, sense spark—the bud.

102 Intelligence

After a cool, refreshing rain, I inhaled fresh, clean and moist air replete with prana. My pranic-work teacher would say to me, "True intelligence resides in the lungs' alveoli." Inhale.

JULIAN LYNN

103 Appearances

"I had a dream that we were all at a party for your mother. I think your mom needs to celebrate something," I suggest while talking on the phone with a friend and fellow yoga instructor.

On the other end of the line, I hear my friend laughing as she responds, "Well, her birthday is two weeks away. Maybe we can plan something to celebrate"

Two weeks pass and preparations are made. A handful of close friends are invited. The element of surprise, when it occurs, is genuine and deeply felt.

The party is grand, not in terms of numbers, but in terms of quality and depth. As a newly formed and closely knit group, we share glorious stories about amazing trips, our closest relationships and unique taste experiences.

YOGA'S DEVOTIONAL LIGHT

When the party ends, everyone leaves feeling heard, nourished and whole.

Then, later on the telephone, my friend reports, "This is really funny; I have to share this with you. Do you remember Diane, my other friend from the party? Well, she said to me later, 'I thought your friend who had the dream would have long flowing hair and wear gathered, full-length skirts or head scarves. She didn't look anything like an intuitive.'"

"My external presentation does not fit society's imagined profile?" I ask. "Maybe I should invest in a head scarf with fake, gold coins? Or, a crystal ball?" There are a few more scenarios with potential costuming variations offered.

"I don't know, but I thought you would find that funny," she laughs.

"The issue of appearances is a strange thing. It is difficult to discern the concerns of others' hearts or learn about their joys, gifts and interests based upon physical appearances alone or a superficial collection of material accoutrements.

"Even speech can be misleading. Sometimes the most apparently verbally and 'socially skilled' individuals are quite unethical. I have experienced this, and it has been painful to observe.

"Anyway," I pause, "I am grateful that you do not need me to carry a crystal ball for the gift of a Divine leading to be taken seriously. And, the party was wonderful."

104 Seers

Children are the true seers, ages two to six, before they become saturated by an excess of worldly experiences or told that they do not understand the world.

105 Tasting Life

    Moving toward an understanding of how our unique, physical system works is sometimes facilitated by moving outside of our well-worn and "comfortable" living patterns. To continue learning and growing means sampling foods we may never have thought of trying, starting a conversation with a safe stranger or pulling on our shoes and traveling to a new neighborhood, city, state or nation.

    Open the door on a new adventure. Keep moving. Taste life.

106 Daffodils

Spring whispers. I hear her, can you?

JULIAN LYNN

107 Dharma

The ahamkara, as the I-maker is sometimes referred to in Sanskrit, is a powerful contender in shaping our lives. When imbalanced, it is the "I, me, mine..." or "I want..." voice of the mind. Yet, it may also function as a bridge to the Self. Many of the roles, we think we want to play in life, come not from our whole or mended hearts but from misguided, social striving or a place of unresolved story.

Several of society's most romanticized roles—that of the great wit, worldly playboy, femme fatale, powerbroker, curmudgeon or sophisticate—may actually involve behavioral components that damage the Spirit, thereby, separating us from following the principles and path (dharma) of our highest Light.

What roles have you been playing?

YOGA'S DEVOTIONAL LIGHT

108 Little Leaf

In Narada's *Bhakti Sutras* (trans. Prem Prakash), aspirants are encouraged to guard and tend to themselves, most especially at the outset of their spiritual journey, as one would a new leaf. We are so very tender, when we first uncover that fragile, first leaf in the heart.

This new leaf has been buried under the protective cover of dried leaves from late, last fall and has survived a long, cold winter. Take care.

109 Present Perfect

Let us not drive the Light away from this singular moment with the coarse sound of empty complaints.

JULIAN LYNN

110 Narrative

All of us have stored narratives—about who we are, who others may be, why something happened or how things came to be. In certain circumstances, personal story can be quite empowering in maintaining healthy boundaries.

If, for example, one thread of my story is "I am a professional," and that narrative keeps me on track at a life-affirming job, then the narrative is assisting me. Often the stories we have developed are quite complex, having unexplored threads, which may sometimes be holding us back from clear perception or keeping us from realizing our potential.

Follow the threads of the stories and beliefs that are holding, and let those leading to tattered hammocks unravel.

YOGA'S DEVOTIONAL LIGHT

111 Inclement

I have a grand pair of traditional puddle boots. We walk together, especially with my canine companions, in weather others would term inclement.

Without the dogs, my boots and I will often stop at a coffee house to take a rest together. When refreshed, we are off on another, new adventure, traversing right through as many puddles as we care to.

112 Float Trip

Riding the current of a river on a float trip, while enjoying incredible scenery, is what genuine, Divine alignment feels like.

JULIAN LYNN

113 Guidance

There is a common misconception that, when we seek clarity during meditation, the Self will produce *the* one answer. In truth, there are multiple life-celebrating and vitality-affirming possibilities. Thus, when we seek clarity during meditation, it is important to be both clear and sure of our intentions.

How broad do we want the positive ripples of our actions, expanding in service to the Self or Self in others, to be? How many people do we want our actions to benefit? How deep should the impact be? These are some of the questions to consider when structuring our queries during contemplative practice and planning our activities for our days.

114 Racing

Observe the racing mind for the toddler that it is. Name each item it picks up, puts down or throws across the room. That calm, patient Observer watching all of the action is your true, internal Guide. Listen to your Self.

115 Inseparable

Yogic Union is like a fireworks' party within the soul, happening without end and all-day long.

Come join us! Pick up a mat. Choose your format. Select a beautiful place for meditation. Start a practice. The display is about to begin.

JULIAN LYNN

116 You and Me

    Vedic texts spend a great deal of time touting meditation as an opportunity to establish a dialogue with "the object" of inquiry. Western readers, steeped in a scientific worldview, may be tempted to think in terms of an implied hierarchy—between the investigator and "the object"—when in fact there should be none. Bumping into righteous indignation, feelings of superiority or self-importance during meditation tells us we have moved away from the heart.

    Wait with an inquiry until you feel delicate tenderness, awe or compassion established again. This tenderness, initially, is so fragile that even a slight breeze seems to scatter a sense of peace.

117 Impressions

Wishing to step into the stream—to connect with all that resonates *Life!*—is not a matter of detaching from the senses but a matter of cleansing them to better receive the inpouring of rich sensory impressions available to us.

118 Kind Care

Never doubt the positive impact that consciously kind speech, actions and choices can have on others. Some recipients of newly thoughtful care and attention may not know, yet, how to receive such kindnesses.

Be patient as old patterns are being reworked. And, as you grow, keep expanding your social circles.

JULIAN LYNN

119 Synchronicities

At the end of a long week, doubt was creeping into my faith in the inherent connectedness of all things sacred and aligned. The wide swatch of magic powder, which feels like it is splashed across my daily life, seemed to have been brushed off or, perhaps, simply worn out.

Never one to doubt the existence of a Supreme Being, or the Divine fabric, and the interwoven nature of all that is holy, I was feeling like my telephone was off the hook, my line was faulty—or, worse, cut.

I run through my check list: A) devotional work; B) formal meditation; C) asana practice (prayer in motion); D) walking in receptive silence. (Clean living is rather a baseline given to receive reliable nudges and leadings; thus, check.) Where is clarity? Where are my nudges?

YOGA'S DEVOTIONAL LIGHT

When all else fails, do a friend a favor, mow the yard or wash laundry.

"I'll do one load of laundry today," I say to myself. I have been out in the woods for a week, and there *is* laundry.

Then, the first nudge comes, "Wait." It is ten o'clock in the morning. I decide to putter around the campsite some more.

Camping is one activity where connectivity almost never fails. Animals are the most aligned creatures I have met. They know what they are supposed to be doing and do it.

At two o'clock in the afternoon, I feel like I should walk up the hill before the day gets away. (This is civilized camping.)

"Wait," comes in again. I set the laundry basket down again. Putter. Putter. Snack. Putter. R-E-L-A-X.

Then, at four o'clock in the afternoon, "Go now." Providence has taught me to be

JULIAN LYNN

timely and punctual. I grab the basket to walk up the hill to the laundry facilities.

At the doorway to the utility room, with one washing machine and one dryer, a gaggle of people are cooing over a dusty, brown puppy. I hear the washing machine already running.

"I must have missed the window in time," I think, consternated with myself.

Then, a woman pipes up from the departing group, "Hey, do you need a free wash? That other woman forgot she had already washed her bedding earlier, and so the washer is ready for you. It has soap and everything in it. Just put your clothing in."

"Really?" comes out of my mouth in surprise and almost involuntarily.

"Yes. Go for it." The bill of her baseball cap shades half of her face and eyes from the sun. She smiles broadly.

Why do I ever doubt?

YOGA'S DEVOTIONAL LIGHT

120 Waxed

Watching a friend wax his sports car, my husband muses, "I wonder if his wife gets that much attention?"

Consider this: How is your time is being spent? Are you creating life-affirming situations? Building and maintaining healthy relationships or tending to an excess of possessions?

121 Oneness

"Goodnight, darling." Dreamless sleep grants us a break from all that separates us from our inherent Oneness—gender, race, age, creed.

Let it all go, and be at peace with your universal Self.

JULIAN LYNN

122 This Is Not Reality

A dim, overcast light filters into my graduate, art-studio space from the skylight above. I am meeting with one of my major faculty advisors to discuss a few sculptural projects, on which I have been working. During the conversation, the broader subject of making art enters our protracted conversation.

"This is *not* reality," he says finally and with conviction. "You know my wife's daughter works for River Cleaners. They staged an environmental action last month where they took an oversized plug in a dinghy 'attempting' to stave off the flow of pollutants from a major chemical plant that has a pipe dumping into the river. There were four or five people bobbing up and down in this little rubber craft in flimsy rain coats, holding a huge plug up next to that pipe, while it dumped harmful chemicals into the waterway. *That* is reality. What we do here is not."

Inside of me, a switch flips with the utterance of that sentence, ending my professional relationship with fine arts, even as I complete my Master's Degree.

This is not reality equals, "This is pretend." Key sentences from this meeting run in a series of loops like an anchoring bassline in music or japa-mantra style. Pulling away from the art world and with the aid of my yoga practice, I begin the process of observing the relationships among people and their things. What I observe amazes me, as the greater Reality is brought to bear.

123 Eden

I can still find Truth in my garden.

JULIAN LYNN

124 Perception

Once we have witnessed the world's luminosity and have had an experience of accurate or clear perception, what keeps us from perpetuating this state of clarity with full appreciation of all that goes on in and around us?

There are four classic, root causes cited for our choosing to continue in various states of misperception: attachment, refusal, fear and ego.

125 Breathing Color

Pungent, rain-soaked colors push their way into the folds of my senses, just as sharp and demanding as unmasked fragrances from the moist earth.

126 Attachment

One of the qualities of misperception (avidya) is our desire to cling to or have an excessive attachment for (raga) the circumstances that produce exquisite or truly extraordinary moments.

Imagine enjoying an exceptional dining experience, where time falls away and everything feels perfect. We are likely to assign our experience to external circumstances: the restaurant, our dining companions or the food. But, what has produced this extraordinary state is in fact the ability we exercised in cultivating internal alignment in order to let go and step into life's flow.

Extraordinary moments are a result of internal alignment, coupled with following through on Divine guidance, not merely accidental happenstance.

JULIAN LYNN

127 Refusal

Life is a plate full of flavors—sweet, sour, salty, bitter or any amalgam. Misperception may result in our wanting to reject or refuse (dves[h]a) flavors we are served. How do we say "yes" to that which *seems distasteful* to the palate? Examine these experiences when in Stillness. Ask, "What do I need from this?" Bitterness may be delivering the very medicine we cannot live without.

128 On a Whim

Rational spontaneity is something born of the Spirit. It is desirable to follow through on positive, sometimes whimsical, and life-affirming desires and actions.

129 Fear

Fearfulness (abhinives[h]a) is the most common, hydra-headed component of misperception. Fear blocks our clear vision of the world—our ability to see the ultimate Reality by causing us to become excessively inward or limited in our perception. Love is stronger than fear.

When we find ourselves in a state of fear, and there is no true danger, or wearing one of fears many masks (anger, righteous indignation, greed, etc.), it is helpful to pause and ask this: What would I do if I were fearless and operating from a generous and fully healed heart?

Opening the door on options, which are not grounded in fear, invites clarity of perception to return.

JULIAN LYNN

130 Ego

Dreamless sleep, in Vedic tradition, is considered one of the most restorative states of being. In dreamless sleep, we are outside of duality—our gender is unknown as are other dualistic emotional and situational states. We experience no conflict in dreamless sleep because we are resting easily in the Self.

During waking hours, as we encounter ego (asmita) and other issues of identity, which may separate us from the Self, it is helpful to tap the strength of the singular perception we receive from our knowledge regarding dreamless sleep. From the seat of Atman, there are neither issues with our personal identity nor are there issues with those who may perceive us as Other. Hold this idea in your heart.

131 Imaginary

There are days when it is easy to grow impatient with people's pettiness. On such days, all we can do, as yoga practitioners, is affirm our connectivity to the Divine and educate people about the imaginary lines we draw that keep us from living in mutual respect for our shared humanity and the Divine Creative Force.

132 Oceans

The distance between the broken heart and the mended heart can feel like an ocean, as we begin sitting for formal meditation. Be assured, that over time, the gap will close. As you seat into your Light, remember to be patient. Visit your cushion as you are able. Be gentle.

JULIAN LYNN

133 Heirloom Seeds

Standing at a swiveling, vertical display of garden-seed packets, a lean man in his sixties approaches the display rack to stand just over my left shoulder. We are both selecting vegetable seeds for spring planting.

Breaking the silence of the selection process, he muses aloud, "It is amazing to think that we are able to buy organic, heirloom seeds in a place like this." We are in the seasonal gardening section of a national, home-improvement chain, surrounded by the ringing, cavernous din unique to that setting.

Turning to face him, I observe, "Producers will respond to the demands of a consumer-based market. Sales are tracked. We are supplied with what we chose to purchase in previous seasons."

YOGA'S DEVOTIONAL LIGHT

"Still, a few years ago this type of selection would not have been possible," he continues to observe.

"We have choices. Our choices drive production and distribution. Consumers, have far more say in and over creating a different future than we might ever imagine. We are in the process of creating tomorrow every day."

"Well, I like that we have these new levels of choice," he announces with optimism. "It bodes well."

134 Time

Receiving assistance boosts the vital energy of both parties—whether we are acting as the doer or the receiver. There is space and time for simple courtesy.

JULIAN LYNN

135 The Homeless I

After class, one of my students approaches me to ask, "Would you consider volunteering just once a week for an hour at the homeless shelter?"

"What would I do?" I ask honestly, while rolling up my yoga mat.

"I would like you to lead a one-hour meditation program with some breathing exercises and simple stretches mixed in," she explains.

"Is there enough interest?" I question.

"I think that we can get a few of the residents to participate, and I know that the staff would benefit greatly. It can get really hectic around there at times."

"Does the shelter accept people who are drunk?" I ask, having seen a handful of students struggle with trying to combine substance usage and the fine-tuning of consciousness—an impossible cocktail for sincere aspirants seeking Union.

She takes a deep breath, clearly apprehensive about her answer changing my willingness to volunteer, "Yes, we accept people who have been drinking. We accept them because they are the most likely to freeze to death when the weather is cold. I think the meditation program should be in the morning or early afternoon so that alcohol is not an issue during that hour."

The woman asking me to volunteer is a favorite student of mine. What she does not know is that, through her inquiry, she has bumped into an uncomfortable and unsorted knot of emotion somewhere in the recesses of my own Spirit.

Because of a family medical situation, we could have easily become homeless ourselves. Thus, my "relationship" with the concept of homelessness and, by extension, homeless people, is a mixed one, involving uninformed ideas about who "they" are (which produces a mild fear of Other) and something akin to an exhaled relief because, "There, but for the grace of God, go I." Facing homelessness directly opens an emotional can of worms.

"Yes. We can try it," I respond, without a lot of conviction. "When would you like for me to come?"

"I work from ten until six on Wednesdays. We could do something in the late morning."

"I could do eleven o'clock on Wednesdays. Would that work?" I ask.

"Yes. Can you start next week?" her face is relaxed again.

"I will see you next Wednesday at eleven o'clock in the morning," I repeat, confirming the day and time.

136 Thread

Delivering surprise roses to one of my community-center yoga students, at her place of work, she says, "You have no idea how challenging my week has been."

During daily meditation, the twin questions: Who am I? And, why am I here? open us to amazing possibilities.

Connecting to the Universal Thread grants each of us the ability to care for one another in unexpected and timely ways. Meditate. Pull the Thread.

137 Umbrella

Walk in the rain and nourish the soft tissues of your body in the moist air.

JULIAN LYNN

138 Fact or Fiction

While exploring the power of story recently, I encountered a circumstance in which someone had a fixed and limiting story about another person of rather intimate acquaintance. This fixed story seemed to be only marginally accurate. But, when it was brought up, as if it were indeed fact, the story's open narration caused the close acquaintance a terrible degree of discomfort, further stifling the hearer's potential growth.

How many times have we held ourselves or another person back through the creation of inaccurate, partially accurate or even accurate but temporal narratives—or inappropriate labels? Why not open to another narrative version of your circumstances or choose new words to describe yourself and your experiences?

YOGA'S DEVOTIONAL LIGHT

139 Walk Forward

Sometimes, it is the very landscape of our past or present emotional experiences, causing us to halt "progress" on our walk forward through linear time. But, in Reality, there is no forward, there is only our current experience of now.

Hatha yoga aids us in reclaiming our personal, earthly vehicle and "retraining" the nervous system, so that a state of contentment may become our new truth.

140 Proof

Science is now verifying or "proving" many things yoga practitioners have long observed. Take time to occupy the laboratory of your own body to find, substantiate and embrace your own Truth.

JULIAN LYNN

141 Social Roles

Ask this question: From which thread in the fabric of my story am I operating when I share information at a party? Do I imagine myself in the role of helper, expert or consultant?

If the receiver is grateful for the information provided, we may be considered helpful and knowledgeable. If, however, our observations are not appreciated, we will be thought of as an intrusive know-it-all.

As yoga practitioners, all we can hope to control, change or redirect are our own thoughts, speech patterns and behaviors. And, the most important thing for us to consider internally is the purity of motivation behind our actions.

What are our intentions?

142 Shall We?

This morning is filled with excitement. I am waiting for the tap on my shoulder from the Light to dance one of my parts in today's Divine parade.

143 Refreshed

Walking among the rain blackened trunks of Friday's trees, the moist air refreshed our bodies. Leaves and skin, bark and pores conveying the renewed air's clarity to all of our internal stirrings.

Simple gratitude.

What a sacred act to be able to breathe fresh, clean and moist spring air.

JULIAN LYNN

144 Saying Yes

Through spiritual practice and many years ago, I met a woman who appeared healthy, but who had active cancer. After our only having met once, she proffered an invitation to my husband and me to come out for a late, evening dinner at her remote homestead, which was a lengthy drive on poor roads and far from town.

We tarried over the decision. And, in a matter of only a few weeks, my new friend was gone.

How often does it happen that one soul asks another soul for some company and the request goes unanswered, disregarded or refused? Love one another, in each moment of every day.

Choose to say, "Yes," to opportunities of community that nourish your Spirit and the Perfection in those around you.

YOGA'S DEVOTIONAL LIGHT

145 consciousness

Late one afternoon, leaving a yoga class with my students, one student looked up and said in enraptured amazement, "The sky! It is as though I have never seen it before."

Inviting clear perception back into our lives is sometimes only a matter of collecting our personal consciousness in and around the body. Then, we can witness creation with renewed senses.

146 Wealth

There were words again about God and riches. "Ah, abundance..." I thought. "Wealth is health and time well spent, among the dearest of our friends."

JULIAN LYNN

147 Memorial Day

There are deep, childhood memories about visiting the graves of distant relatives in small-town cemeteries on Memorial Day weekend.

Much of what we do, whether it is honoring those who have passed before us or going through our ordinary routines, involves the structuring or configuration of our identities. Yet, from the space of our hearts, there is a universal brightness which delivers wonder and awe to each of our interactions and connections.

Take a universal perspective along to a family gathering this holiday weekend, and mend, perhaps, one old relationship in a state of disrepair.

Compassion is the most reliable vehicle for traveling.

YOGA'S DEVOTIONAL LIGHT

148 Simplicity

When the heart is filled to brimming and we have realized the bottomless nature of Life's cup, then, and only then, will surrender, renunciation and simple living come to equal the fullness of unstoppable gratitude and joy.

149 Higher Ground

I found a picture book of India recently, featuring photographs of the country in all seasons.

During the monsoons, whole villages find refuge from the flooding on the tracks of India's vast railway system's higher ground. Are we not all looking for the safer, higher ground?

JULIAN LYNN

150 The Homeless II

Arriving at the homeless shelter, I am met by a wall of noise. Doors are constantly banging as people move in and out. The phone rings, and there are multiple loud conversations going on across the main room. Shelter guests help each other at computers, with resumés, spelling and email, as well as swapping job leads and the names of the city's best resources and physicians.

"How in the world are we going to meditate in here?" I wonder to myself.

I check in with my student, who is the manager on duty. She smiles as I approach her desk, picking up the phone to take another incoming call.

"Where are we planning to set up to do this?" I ask her.

"I think that we can do it right here—in the big room. A lot of people will be clearing out to grab sack lunches at some of the local churches," she reassures me.

Within ten minutes, we have a circle of benches arranged, and the big room has indeed become quieter. Soon, the program is live, and I am playing to a crew of about six people.

After brief introductions, we practice some breathing exercises, designed to balance brain activity. Next, I lead everyone through a few simple chair stretches. In doing this, what I learn is that most participants are somehow physically disabled, and many of them are former construction workers or laborers. I am amazed at the information coming out: smashed knee caps, dislocations, broken bones with plates, screws and wires holding everything together. It feels like I am at a hardware convention.

JULIAN LYNN

When one man falls slightly behind, he informs me, "We are with ya sister. Ya know we wouldn't be here except that we're all broke up; and, because of that, we have been tossed out."

The hour wraps up with a few minutes of meditative silence and a great deal of squirming. I make a note to keep things focused on active participation—counted breathing and stretches. The space is too kinetic for a long, formal meditation, though everyone seems to be enjoying the peaceful oxygen "buzz" that accompanies deep breathing and a proper, yogic reboot.

"Same time next week?" my student asks, standing up from the bench.

"Yes, I will be here."

On the way home, I ponder the harsh irony that the majority of homeless men I met today were former construction workers. Can we not find housing for the people who did the building?*

*Later, I learn that for some men, at least at this shelter, the cycle goes something like this: Married, wife with kids, good paychecks, family picnics and beer on weekends. Then, accident at work, disability, radically reduced income, no picnics—with pain and beer all week long. Eventually, no wife or kids.

A permanent, physical place of residence or "home" for a single, disabled man may seem pointless, emotionally empty—and, on disability, unaffordable.

When considering the issue of establishing stable residences for the homeless, we need to remember that homelessness is a complex issue involving issues of health, disability, medication—pharmaceutical and street versions—cognitive function, mental health, chronically low wages and strained family relationships and situations. It is important to leave judgment behind.

JULIAN LYNN

151 Mending

Meditation is capable of assisting us in mending past injuries. After passing through a phase of personal "indulgence" and resolution, a delta opens to the universal ocean of Peace, where we want nothing more than to give or share with others. Board the lifeboat, which meditation offers, and take the trip.

152 Wonder

Touching the Reality, which is holy, is a matter of hunkering down in the body to observe with amazement the natural pageantry all around—from a seat with an exceptional view. Strut, dance and live in wonder. Divine Mother provides us with the partners we need.

153 Ideas

We are so much more than the body, being neither tall nor short, lean nor round, strong nor weak, healthy nor compromised—nor any other external, physical attribute. Yet, how we choose to care for our earthly home of genetic issue reveals a great deal about our life experiences, emotional states of being and attitudes toward physicality.

Have you fueled your sacred vehicle today? Washed and buffed your holy carriage? Lubed your chassis? Scheduled your regular maintenance?

In Vedanta, if we were to boil philosophical ideas down, we might take one of three world views toward living this earthly life:

The physical realm is an illusion—a mask—covering the luminescence of the ultimate Reality and beauty of the Supreme Spiritual Realm.

Or, the physical realm is as real as the nonphysical, Spiritual realm, but the Spiritual realm is of far, far greater importance.

Or, finally, all realms emanate from Source, with the physical realm having been expressly created so that Source might delight in the totality of Her rich, broad and profound Creation.

This final model invites us to respect and delight in our singular place in the world, as well as asking us to look upon our bodies as holy vehicles. We must take special care with the whole of ourselves.

The world becomes a place of wonder, when we hold the body to be sacred and the physical manifestations of Source's many other forms (other bodies), no matter how different those physical frames appear to be from our own.

YOGA'S DEVOTIONAL LIGHT

How different our days become when we hold this idea in our hearts and when we respect each other as aspects of the Divine, or as sacred components in the Divine creative plan.

154 Breath of Joy

Sip an inhale, sweeping your straight arms up in front of your body and overhead (palms should face one another); sip an inhale while sweeping your arms out to each side—at shoulder height; sip an inhale sending your arms up and overhead again. (The movement should look like that of an orchestra conductor.) Take a long exhale, sending both arms straight down to your sides, while bending gently at the hips and knees. Repeat: three sips, one full exhale. This is, indeed, a most rejuvenating practice.

JULIAN LYNN

155 Complete

In connecting with our essence, we may notice cravings for less-than-optimal stimuli and "extraordinary experiences" give way to the desire for an unbroken, internal Peace.

Searches and wishes for heightened experiences are often driven by a sense of incompleteness or emptiness that seems filled by short-term gratification, entertainment or an adrenaline rush.

Union fills completely; so that the experiences we have, while seated in our wholeness, become magical, affirming the very sanctity of our individual existence. The need for certain external stimuli may end up falling away entirely. Or, if indulged in, it is done with ceremonial respect or form.

Go ahead. Invite change. Evolve.

YOGA'S DEVOTIONAL LIGHT

156 Pleasures

In *The Upanishads*, pleasure is described as a positive sense experience occurring as a result of touch, taste, smell, seeing or hearing. Pleasures are fleeting and, in cases when they are visited excessively, may lead to an insatiability of appetite, as well as wild fluctuations in an otherwise smoothly running mind.

157 Joys

In contrast to pleasure, joy is the emotion most often experienced by yogis grounded in their practice and in the Self. Joys well naturally in the free and unfettered heart of any devotee, within any religion, who is committed to service.

JULIAN LYNN

158 Expansion

Having spent much of the day in meditation, I am out for a lengthy walk to revisit the space of my body. It is a beautiful, late summer evening.

Walking through a section of town, where I do not usually wander on foot, I observe more closely the incredible trees, on a broad boulevard, extending their generous branches across the closest of lanes. The trees separate four lanes of traffic near a newly renovated city park. The umbrella, which the trees' canopies form, places a protective veil of nature over what would otherwise be a rather stark urban setting in concrete.

Heading toward a mature adolescence, the trees' arbor is already substantial. City planners have taken special care in designing the boulevard to accommodate for the trees' growth. Yet, the trees' roots are cramped beneath the concrete road, as they bulge above the designated apron of earth provided to them.

So fresh from the meditation cushion, I can feel the trees' mild grief with their urban placement, as if it is carried in the evening breeze. The tree branches and leaves move, creating a whispered chant like that of an ancient Greek chorus.

And, I respond to the trees' rustling song, "Sisters, how graciously you serve us and how thoughtlessly we proceed."

In the *Taittiriya Upanishad*, we are reminded that the Self is in the sun and within all Beings. That Self is the same, unchangeable and immutable. There is Oneness and Unity in life, available to each of us, when we shed all sheaths.

JULIAN LYNN

159 care

The care of a friend's receptive heart touches the deepest of injuries once sequestered in our own hard-working muscle. Tender care is one of the greatest sources of personal strength: Friendship + Love = Heart Repair.

160 Moment

Only an unsettled mind argues about the perfection of a given moment when there is no strife present. Carry peace within yourself and rise in the morning with the angels, walk throughout the day with saints and bask in your connectivity to the pulse of Life.

YOGA'S DEVOTIONAL LIGHT

161 Growing

It is June, and the weather is unusually cool and sumptuous. The rains are uncommonly frequent. By night, seeming to be sprinkled with magical faerie dust, the garden grows wildly.

We have been enjoying salads with rainbow chard, turnip greens and romaine, as well as homemade tahini, lemon juice and dill-weed dressing. (Mix the tahini with a little boiling water first to gain the consistency.)

What a wonder the natural world is. Gardening leads to an appreciation for those who make farming their way of life. After a season of growing a few of our personal vegetables, a full plate of food is nothing short of a glorious miracle.

JULIAN LYNN

162 Possibilities

Over dinner and after a full evening of storytelling with a new friend, I said, "We will need to space out our meetings, so we do not run out of material."

She looked at me with sly amusement, saying, "We will never run out of material. We are individuals of infinite possibility and endless stories."

163 Pampered

The human organism is home while we are here. Solid self-care includes tending to the body, and it may function as the first step toward growing compassion, charity and forgiveness toward those whom we might initially consider Other.

164 Giving Bowl

   Offering up morning devotions, my breathing becomes even. There is still no clear nudge on plans for the day. We are observing silence at home. The quiet space of silence allows the dust of emotions and thoughts to settle so that the pure kernel in my heart may appear with a damp dusting cloth to wipe away unresolved confusion or recent pain. Silence also grants each of us the space we need, away from verbal transactions, to listen for the subtle cues on how to move forward with guidance—on any given day.

   Taking a break from my meditation cushion, I walk out onto the back deck to see that my husband has mowed the yard again. This is an act of courtesy for our neighbors, who are celebrating their marriage at their home, with visiting

JULIAN LYNN

extended family. The newly trimmed lawn makes me feel like landed gentry. In my gratitude for the green space and on the exhale outside, clarity comes.

Back inside the house, I pull out my laptop and compose the following note for our newlywed neighbors:

This is The Giving Bowl

Every marriage must have a great deal of positive interaction, play, fun and forgiveness built into it. The Giving Bowl is designed to aid in this process.

These are instructions on how to use this gift. Keep the bowl anywhere you would like. When you have something positive to share, give or communicate to your partner, take it down and place the bowl (and the slip of paper or object) in a location where the other person may easily find it. Here are just a few sample items to place in the bowl:

A breakfast bar;
A coupon for a foot massage;
A coupon for a kitchen clean-up;
Five dollars for a cup of tea;
A note: "Thank you for mowing.
　　　　　The lawn looks great."

Your own kindness and imagination set the limit. Have fun with it!

In the gift corner of our house, there is a covered bowl that serves perfectly. Wrapping that bowl in a box, I tape the note, which I have printed, into a card and onto the top of the wrapped package.

As I prepare to walk next door, another nudge from the Self stops me, "The bag in the closet."

From the coat closet, I pull out a plain, crumpled paper grocery bag. Inside there is a new designer handbag. It is beautifully made. (Every girl should have one thing in her possession that makes her feel

JULIAN LYNN

extraordinary.) I walk over to the neighbors' home with not one but two gifts in hand. It is a beautiful summer day.

With dogs barking a greeting next door, I announce, "I have brought one gift for Angela and Mark. The unwrapped gift is for Angela alone." Everyone is still in pajamas as the gifts are handed off. The wedding involved a late-night party.

Walking home, I feel the lightness that comes from following the wise leadings of my heart supported by pure intention. The day has already been so kind.

165 Observing

With our internal Observer established, it is easier to choose when, where and with whom we should be extending ourselves. Ask yourself this question: How do I become my best me?

166 Body Machine

Exhale. Inhale and raise all ten toes. Exhale. Then, inhale while flexing both hands and lifting and opening the chest, with an expansive and deep breath. Continue breathing deeply.

Beautiful, poetic body machine, you are perfect! Repeat.

167 Rescued

Through contemplative practice, as we begin to unmask our Light, the baldness of our past errors may cause us to want to put our meditation cushion away in the recesses of a long, dark closet. Yet, as we continue to sit, assistance will show up in the form of emotional Graces. Trust.

JULIAN LYNN

168 Awakening

The practice of sense withdrawal (pratyahara) in yoga is sometimes touted as a pinnacle experience, where we are then expected to reside on an elitist mountain, forever rejecting the "lower" sense engagements

Experience teaches many of us that emerging from a conscious phase of sense withdrawal, causes us to savor—with renewed awareness and gratitude—the bounty which Divine Mother places consistently before us.

Thus, sense withdrawal becomes a means by which we may foster additional gratitude for life's small details and simplest of joys. And, ultimately, we will feel a push to expand and share that sense of bounty with others.

169 Unchained

Does the intention come from a seat of purity? Purity sounds like a far and away, distant concept, but it is not. Purity comes from an unchained heart.

An unchained heart is inherently supportive and kind. An unchained heart reaches out to touch others' lives when they are in need and most especially when surplus is at hand. An unchained heart takes care of itself in the best ways possible. This is the secret behind sharing simple kindnesses with one another.

170 Lullaby

When was the last time you made up a short song? Before dozing off tonight, sing your gratitude list. Sleep in peace.

JULIAN LYNN

171 Awareness

In teaching, there is a concept known as setting the tone, in which teachers are made aware of the fact that a group of impressionable students and young minds are inclined to take on the emotional attitude or personality of the person leading the class—the teacher.

This concept is not limited to the teacher-student relationship in schools or other academic settings, but it also has an impact on group dynamics whenever there is a designated leader-group relationship.

Whether we are in the role of teacher or student, manager or coworker, we need to be aware of the primary attitude or complex of attitudes we are taking with us into our environments. And, most especially, if we are in the role of hatha-yoga teacher and working through issues of latent anger or frustration, we must be self-aware enough that we do not attempt to resolve our emotional issues by pushing a room full of trusting students through an excessively rigorous asana class.

Outside of group dynamics, the best application of setting the tone comes when we learn to apply this concept to our individual, internal development. Each personality is multifaceted, possessing a variety of presentations—most especially when we are not yet practiced in being able to reside fully seated in the Self.

Try utilizing the concept of setting the tone *within* yourself first, making your highest Light your leader or teacher figure. Such an application of this principle usually lends itself to a more reliable unfolding of internal events and the personality's coupling with the inherent integrity and truth residing in the heart.

JULIAN LYNN

Summer

172 Attainments

The "attainments" (siddhis) are gifts stemming from a still, reflective mind in coordinated action with the Divine Creative Force. They are to be received quietly and graciously, without heraldry or flaunting. Individuals of devotion, profound faith and consistent alignment describe having these gifts visited upon them—no matter what one's religious, spiritual or philosophical affiliation.

173 Child

Honoring our internal, sacred child is what allows us to serve as spiritual adults with dignity, consistency, ease and Grace.

JULIAN LYNN

174 Approval

Getting quiet enough to listen for and follow the urgings of the Self, in alignment with our perception of Divine will, can be challenging, daily work.

However, the greater challenge may be moving forward, in the context of society at large, with actions in support of simple living and in support of yogic principles. The pressure to conform, which society may bring to bear upon us, is broader than we might initially imagine.

Over time, our external need for social approval begins to fall away, being supplanted by the heart's tender relationship with the One, eternal Truth.

Trust that Truth and move without injuring yourself or moving into judgment about those around you.

175 Expansiveness

Passing through the Great Plains, there is an expansiveness to the landscape giving the earth and sky a feeling of limitlessness. Waves of gratitude roll out for the farm families committed to the hard work of farming and for their willingness to feed us all. Namaste!

176 Immense

Bumping up against our immensity is daunting because it requires a complete reframing of answers to the questions: Who am I? And, why am I here?

Fear about our "bigness" is the primary thing holding most of us back. Do not be afraid to embrace your immensity. It comes prepackaged with humbleness.

JULIAN LYNN

177 Receiving

    The attainments (siddhis) present something of a challenge for any Western teacher or practitioner of contemplative practices. They are gifts so extraordinary, rare and precious that they should be held closely and quietly inside of us.

    One challenge, to a Western recipient of any such gift, is that—in most normal circumstances—we are without the guidance or training to contextualize or even name what is happening. With care, these gifts, which are far from being the paranormal phenomena of Western psychology, assist us in serving as we walk our spiritual path—just as aspects of our regular practices guide us through our daily lives and activities.

178 Humidity

    The weather is warm and moist—sauna days; so perfect for the first few days of summer. Only the pups are brokenhearted about not being able to tag along during in-vehicle errands. The car grows far too hot under the sun.

    On the upside, there is free hot yoga on the grass in the backyard!

179 Lighthouse

    To stand steady, a lighthouse at the edge of rough seas, polish brass, shine mirrors and keep the fire in your lamp alive—in Stillness and while circling a full three-hundred-and-sixty degrees.

    Then, you may be able to assist others, wishing to arrive safely ashore.

JULIAN LYNN

180 Noble Travelers

   In my childhood, my grandmother told stories about her growing up in a large home several blocks from the community's sole railroad depot. My great-grandfather, a railroad supervisor, liked to walk to work.

   Because of their home's proximity to the depot, my grandmother's family saw and served hobos, who rode the empty boxcars. My grandmother's home was marked as a place, where—to use the Taoist term—"noble travelers" could receive an exceptional meal in exchange for completing a chore. (The chopping of extra firewood for cooking and baking was always appreciated by the household.)

   So, when my husband comes home one evening from a walk, it does not surprise me to see him toting a woolen blanket in need of a good washing. He has picked it up after helping a homeless veteran find a safe place to bed down for the night.

"Hey, put the blanket on the back porch. Maybe don't come through the house again? If it rains, we will get some needed help with a prewash," I say, looking up from writing.

I am a rather unusual bird in that I am a Laundromat enthusiast. Although we could purchase a washer and dryer (and it would be more economical), I like to frequent public Laundromats for a variety of reasons. Here are a few:

1. Efficiency. I love getting everything washed in industrial-sized machines all at once. And, commercial machines seem to extract better than in-home models, thus drying time is shorter.

2. Personal space. A trip to the Laundromat is an opportunity for contemplation and reading time.

JULIAN LYNN

I finally have an excuse to read the glossy magazines. (This is where I drop our own subscriptions, which I do not have time to read at home.)

3. Interesting people. The wide variety of people I meet is educational and many seem to need kind thoughts and words. (I almost always return home with new gratitude for my circumstances.)

4. Getting out. Writing and meditation are mostly solo activities. Moving into community pulls me out of my personal, conceptual world, planting me solidly again on planet earth. This is Laundromat as village watering hole.

Back to blankets. As it turns out, that first blanket is the kick off for a new phase in our household's devotional practice. (My husband and I sometimes work in tandem.) For several months, we launder, fold and roll now clean blankets into plastic bags, attaching notes to indicate that they are clean and ready for use. My husband does the field work.

And, because we are on track in universal terms, by meeting a need in the community, abandoned or discarded woolen blankets simply start to appear. *Providence provides, when we are in a state of alignment with Divine will.*

At some point, I go through our closets, downsizing and donating our existing excess inventory of linens, giving those items to the local transitional housing facility for the homeless.

Then, things shift. We feel nudged to serve in other ways. This is the nature of dharma. Expect and accept change.

Put your ear to the tracks. Listen. And, with an open and receptive heart, ask about the manner in which you are *currently* meant to serve. It is by asking that you will know how to proceed.

JULIAN LYNN

181 Lighter than Air

Levitation is the attainment which is the making of great legends, magicians and mythical figures. Have you ever had the experience of being in a state where you feel like you are walking on clouds?

This is the emotional levitation that occurs with a profound experience of Union, an exceptional practice or when someone, in a deep state of Love, makes a commitment from a seat of devotion, which is in complete alignment with his very essence and Universal principles.

This form of levitation is authentic and pregnant with the gift of spiritual upliftment, capable of carrying us over ordinary obstacles and through time.

182 Inside

When we spend time focusing on appearances, we tend to forget what we really desire—consistent exchanges of mutual integrity. This is all that our hearts really want. Close your eyes and look past another person's surface appearance to embrace what is being expressed by that person's internal Light.

183 Holiday Boom

Celebrating life and holidays with explosive volume? We must remember our furry, four-legged friends. More joy and comfort will be enjoyed by all, if they are in a safe place, away from the din.

JULIAN LYNN

184 Disappearing

One of the most extraordinary of the attainments, for any modern to conceptualize, is the notion of invisibility. How does an adept make herself effectively disappear at will?

This gift is readily granted to any aspirant on the path whenever we choose to make an anonymous donation or when we engage in generous acts of anonymous kindnesses. "Disappearing at will" is a matter of releasing the ego by releasing the desire to be known or recognized.

So, go ahead and disappear. We are each fully capable of becoming invisible patrons, angels and generous sponsors, working to acknowledge the hearts, lives and needs of those around us.

185 Patience

Just as the weather, during seasonal transitions, feels capricious bouncing between highs and lows so, too, does the heart feel capricious during phases of serious remodel, or when fully gutted for complete reconstruction.

The new plan is worth the wait. It will be extraordinary.

186 Inside Out

Living meditation is something we take with us, when we wash the car in the driveway, pick up our children after school or help a stranger spontaneously.

Calm awareness is available, as we carry the Self forward into the context of a very busy, social and physical world.

JULIAN LYNN

187 Flexibility

Another attainment describes us as having the ability to become as small as an atom or as expansive as the universe. In considering this gift, it is helpful to recall the social situations we move through, where, depending upon our role, we may be practicing this ability already.

Ask these questions: Was I an attentive, quiet listener or an expansive host? Am I able to play both parts with equal dignity? We have all practiced this.

Atom or universe?

As yoga practitioners, we learn to cultivate the ability (and flexibility) to step into the role or roles that are most situationally fitting and luminescent for us.

Next time a social situation allows, explore expansion and contraction.

188 Give Away

My blue, cotton sunhat changed hands today. During my long walk, when I came across a woman behind a stroller with an infant, wearing nothing but a diaper, I asked about protection.

The woman apologized, "I've been trying to walk in the shade."

These were the words of genuine embarrassment from behind the diaper-only baby and stroller, as I handed off my freshly laundered hat.

189 High Winds

Serious weather reminds us that the human frame is a vehicle—both frail and strong, delicate and resilient.

JULIAN LYNN

190 Given

In his use of the Sanskrit word siddhi, T.K.V. Desikachar uses the English word "given" rather than the more commonly used translations of the attainments, accomplishments or, in Buddhism, perfections. Something that is given is an unexpected gift. Gifts are not to be strived for, chased after or achieved, but received with humble gratitude.

The siddhis are delivered to us or occur naturally when all conditions are appropriate. It is usually when we move in the direction of selfless service and are no longer seeking the siddhis, that they appear unannounced, like little gifts in ornately wrapped boxes, left anonymously on a freshly-swept, front doorstep.

YOGA'S DEVOTIONAL LIGHT

191 Yoga Nidra

Yoga nidra or yogic sleep is said to be a more effective form of resetting the body than some forms of sleep. Yogic sleep involves the conscious restoration of the body's systems. Move with your consciousness through your body, inviting the body to reset itself.

192 Archeology

When our minds are allowed to run free, the wild stories we have sequestered away about ourselves and others are exposed. Unearth these inconsistent and potentially dangerous narrative artifacts; then, release them by observing things as they are in real time. This is Presence.

JULIAN LYNN

193 Mind Reading

"Knowing the thoughts of others" is the classical mind-reader attainment. This gift asks us to be aware of what is going on around us with regard to others' comforts and discomforts, begging us to take action according to our abilities.

The Dalai Lama embodied this gift, during a speaking presentation in Birmingham, Alabama, when he became aware of the Mayor's discomfort under the hot sun. Stopping his talk before hundreds of people, the Dalai Lama graciously extended the Mayor his personal shade umbrella before continuing his talk.

Look around. We have the capability of cultivating this type of awareness through keen observation and by taking actions to reduce the discomfort of others with the simplest of actions of genuine goodwill.

YOGA'S DEVOTIONAL LIGHT

194 Providence

    After observing several months of guided, selfless service—by laundering and placing clean blankets out in plastic bags with little notes for the area's homeless people—I observe a marked shift in the prattle going on in my mind during a walk home from the grocery store. (Observing internal dialogue is one of the best methods for a balanced person to use in determining continued appropriateness of path and action.)

    Monitoring my mind's one-sided conversation, I note I have clearly stepped away from that plane of humble gratitude for the gift of service, where I usually live, and have entered the dangerous high seas of self-pity, doubt and social preoccupation, leading to a head-on

JULIAN LYNN

collision with the dread pirates—Frustration, Anger and Materialism.

The prattle goes something like this: So, who am I? The laundress for the homeless? And, how am I supposed to afford the new under things I need, when we are being nickeled-and-dimed with all of this extra laundry? Also, I have pretty much had it with the pathetic treatment I have been receiving at the hands of the so-called religious people, who only seem to care about social appearances. But, what do I know?

Amid the blazing one-sided cannons, which I have rolled out, and the unraveling of my internal frustrations, a gentle push to cross four-lanes of traffic in an unusual location comes through, "Cross here."

My mind is still knitting itself into a straightjacket of fiery complaint as I walk on the diagonal underneath a railroad overpass. Stopping between the third and fourth lanes, with my dogs, I scoop up the answer to my entreaties: two brand-new brassieres half out of their packaging—obviously discarded—and not yet driven over. The brassieres are not only in a style I wear, but they are *IN MY SIZE*.

"Ask and ye shall receive," my mind sputters to a halt as emotional awe and wonder for the Divine hand returns.

Approaching the table of peace and reconciliation again, I renew my vows to practice listening, prayerful diplomacy and walking in a state of gratitude for the opportunities of service Providence grants.

195 Harsh People

Some crusty, harsh people are akin to old-fashioned, hard fruit candies with liquid centers of pure delight, filled with incredible bursts of flavor. Be patient.

JULIAN LYNN

196 Shared Minds

Early explorers of the Americas noted that some native peoples engaged in a practice called dream walking. In yogic tradition, dream walking is one of the gifts. By definition, it is the joining of one person's consciousness with that of another during meditation or dream time in order to communicate something of importance.

More critical than the development of or desire for such an attainment are the questions that such a skill begs to ask: With whom should I share my dream time or consciousness? And, with whom would I like to walk my path? In truth, we already possess shared consciousness, especially in our most immediate and intimate relationships.

197 care

While riding my bicycle to the library, I meet a cardboard-recycling, truck driver, as he personally loads his semi with a forklift. He politely warns me about the hot, hot weather.

I thank him, saying, "Bicycling in the heat is like driving the quietest convertible possible. The breeze makes riding incredibly comfortable."

What a charitable act—to have a stranger concerned about my well-being.

198 Moment

Stop. Pause now. Shift focus to the quality of your breathing to cultivate healthy beginner's mind, opening a door on *this* moment.

JULIAN LYNN

199 Past Lives

For many Westerners, an occurrence of past-life recall is most likely to happen in the context of dream time, when we experience a theme mirroring our current life circumstances but with a different set of costumes and a few changes to the cast of characters surrounding us.

Having an experience of this gift is best treated like the viewing of an allegorical play. What drama or farce may we be repeating? Must it be played out the same way? We may not always exercise it, but we have a tremendous amount of freewill.

There are daily opportunities to rewrite the script we are living—to become more patient or kinder and to choose to speak out and care for one another in ways we would not have had the courage to do in the past.

YOGA'S DEVOTIONAL LIGHT

200 Weather

    Incredible outside conditions may create for us momentary, emotional joy about existing in the world. External weather, however, is often changeable and can be highly variable. Thus, being able to create our own "internal weather" conditions, which are to our liking, is a highly desirable ability.

    The siddhi which describes being impervious or indifferent to hunger, thirst, heat and cold reminds us that we are capable of fostering this ability through a consistent relationship with our Atman—the sacred Self.

    What internal weather conditions would you create? Hold steady in your intentions for this potential.

JULIAN LYNN

201 Tao of Yoga

Remaining "unconquered by others" is an elusive gift. It encourages the practice of non-attachment, teaching us to give, receive and live selflessly, according to our meditative clarity, as we wade amid life's social flow. Imagine living in a perfectly balanced ecosystem, where we are able to give and receive what we need from a fully compassionate heart.

202 Green Space

Green space presents us with the greatest respite from our worldly preoccupations, offering up solutions as we walk, garden, play and sky gaze.

203 Manifesting

The materialization of objects or desires is a common topic of conversation among some students of consciousness. The external objects we think we need are usually stand-ins for intangible qualities or traits where we perceive ourselves to be deficient. Thus, the luxury car may be a physical stand-in for an issue of status. Dreams of an exotic vacation might stem from feelings about a lack of leisure or issues of privilege.

When meditating, try leaving desire or "I want" open ended, allowing Source to fill your perceived needs. Opportunities and gifts, thus granted, are far richer, greater and more fulfilling than any physical object we could possibly receive.

JULIAN LYNN

204 Elements

One of the siddhis of legend is being able to control or check the influence of certain elements. These are not the elements of the periodic chart, but the traditional elements of many ancient philosophical systems: sun, earth, wind, water or fire.

Rather than thinking about bending or changing the external world to fit the desires of our personal will, in considering this gift, it is best to focus first on how we respond internally to external stimuli.

Once we become unflappable, the external elements will cease to have control over us. An experience and knowledge of the immutable Self is required. Again, the work is internal.

205 Hope

There is an external, physical appearance to scenes, people and objects. Then, there is the "internal" or essential, spiritual Reality of scenes, people and objects. The disparity between these two points of view can, at times, be great indeed. The practiced yogi, grounded in the Self, knows which to be true.

206 Vital Signs

What if every decision we made had to take into account how it would impact our own or another's personal vitality?

What if we respected one another enough to refrain from harming the Self, as well as another's physical frame?

JULIAN LYNN

207 Departure

In Western scientific literature, some people report feeling like they are suspended above their bodies during a physical trauma or a major surgery, indicating they only enter the physical vessel again after the body is deemed safe enough for renewed inhabitation.

In Vedic tradition, leaving the body at will or detaching from the senses is one of the attainments. Gandhi is said to have refused anesthetic for a surgery, choosing instead to detach from the senses of his physical frame while the whole of the procedure was performed.

In one version of utopia, we would create a world where everyone wants to be embodied and fully present.

208 Layers in Time

Seeing past, present and future is a less common gift. In approaching such experiences, the lessons such sight provides, in current time, are the most valuable as we watch the timeline of life float through our consciousness.

What pattern of behavior, emotion or relationship are we being asked to retain or reconfigure? What archetypal roles do we assume most consistently? Would another set of behaviors or roles be healthier for us and for those around us?

We, as individuals, possess an amazing degree of freewill, which continues to go unexercised. To what do we say, "Yes, or no?" Diplomacy allows us to move easily across the stage of this theatre.

JULIAN LYNN

209 sliding

On my tenth or twelfth time down the water slide at the municipal pool, the lifeguard says, "You look like you are having a blast."

"I am—must be on the right path. Your path should bring you joy." And, then, with a watery wink, I continue, "Don't let anyone keep you from your joy."

Dripping, I fly down the slide again.

210 sing!

Music most certainly opens the ready heart, wishing to embark on a spiritual journey. Listen, play, tap, drum, dance, wiggle, hum and sing! You are vibrating.

211 Intention & Trust

Conceptually, I live on a rare corner of the linguistic earth, where the vocabularies of several spiritual traditions coalesce. It is like a lookout point, showcasing a place on the map where the boundaries of several different states meet. The understanding that comes from this vantage point is that edges or "boundaries" are created for human convenience.

I arrived at this location because of the trek I took to understand who I am, why I am here and how I am meant to live and serve. Clarity is derived from my contemplative practices, helping me answer the questions I pose during my daily raja yoga practice—about how best to proceed on any given day.

Thus, one day, while sitting in meditation, a note is dropped into my

metaphorical inbox, "Pack your suitcase."
(I have learned, the hard way, to heed these subtle meditative nudges.)

So, after meditation, I dutifully pull out my small suitcase. Because the thread of meditation is still humming, I make a quick inquiry about how long I might be gone and am guided to pack for ten days. Upon finishing, I set my suitcase into an empty corner of my room with a feeling of anticipation. I like small trips.

The next day, as I send out careful feelers during meditation, this comes through, "The healing has occurred."
(e.g. "You do not have to travel for this.")

All at once, I experience a wave of various emotional responses: mild joy—because I do not have to leave my comfortable, domestic routines; disappointment—because I do enjoy reasonable trips, and I was so looking forward to going "somewhere" to do

YOGA'S DEVOTIONAL LIGHT

"something" for "someone;" frustration—because, when I am in my cranky, lower-self, I still occasionally feel batted about by Providence, albeit for sacred purposes (after all, I reason, I did put time into packing); AMAZEMENT—because Source continues to fill me with awe and wonder when the holy gust of pure intention sweeps into my life and sets things right, because I was and am willing to pack my suitcase in service to the Divine and go on an errand for which I do not have a name, place, person or stated case of concern.

Be of good intention and good cheer. No pure intention is in vain.

212 Abandon

Just once today—do something with the full abandon of a child.

JULIAN LYNN

213 Turning

 Sitting three cars back from a stop sign, in my vehicle on the edge of a parking lot, I am waiting impatiently to enter six lanes of busy traffic.

 Mentally, I drum my fingers on the steering wheel. The tattoo of my consciousness thumps, "Come on. Come on. Me. Me. Me. I am late. Repeat."

 Suddenly and from the far right, the blaring scream of a racing ambulance breaks into my consciousness, along with a complete shift in my frame of mind.

 "Where is my compassion?" I ask.

 I stop the flow of "I, me and mine" to request that those, who are in need of emergency assistance, please receive optimal care in a timely fashion. Then, I ask the Powers-That-Be to guard, guide and protect the responders, helping them

YOGA'S DEVOTIONAL LIGHT

make solid decisions as they serve those involved in the emergency. Time slows. Impatience evaporates. Peace settles in.

Releasing a false sense of self-importance allows the world to open and, it would seem, Eternity to flow in.

214 Deep Roots

Contemplative students worry about overindulging their newly rediscovered internal child. Play a little, indulge your innocence and watch that it is not inflated ego at work. This will allow you to heal properly and move forward. Be bright.

You will be so much stronger, if you allow for your own healing by honoring both your internal child and mature Light.

JULIAN LYNN

215 Balance

Physical practice offers us the potential to strengthen the body. The hope is that we will reduce our experiences of fatigue and illness, a block to mental clarity as described in the *Yoga Sutra*, and be able to host the Self, in the context of a supple, healthy physical frame.

Many hatha-yoga practitioners do enjoy generally healthier bodies, because yoga teaches us to read the frame's subtle cues for maintaining our personal well-being with increasing accuracy.

Then, if we are on the edge of some illness, we are better able to apply "remedies" of, perhaps, more sleep, improved nutrition, gentle movement, rest or laughter to keep us moving toward vibrancy and Union.

216 High Society

At a formal dinner party, I am pressed for information about "where" I live. I want to reply, "I attempt to live from the space of my sacred heart. And, you? Where do you live?"

Be at home in your heart.

217 Balancing

Alternate nostril breathing (nadi s[h]odhana) is one of Vedic traditions most effective practices, aiding us in cleansing the body's energetic channels (nadis) and producing a balanced, internal calm that cannot be surpassed. Seek a qualified instructor and appropriate instruction.

JULIAN LYNN

218 At-ONE-ment

"You can never wear too much purple," is how the conversation starts. The woman at the deli and two tables away notices my layering of fashion-camping don'ts. (I had sneaked into a small town, without regard to my clothing's appearance, to check email.)

While we are enjoying a lively verbal volley, a man comes to join her at her small table. Then, more pointed questions ensue from both of them.

"Who are you?" (A writer.)

"What do you write about?" (Spirituality, yoga, well-being and experiences of sacred Union.)

"What is the most important yoga posture?" (S[h]avasana.)

YOGA'S DEVOTIONAL LIGHT

"Why?" (This posture offers the potential for an experience of unbroken Peace or at-one-ment.)

Then, more distinctly, the gentleman intones, "Aaaahh, that is what I have been missing—at-ONE-ment." Laughter. (You should pick up one of my books.)

This is how two strangers become two dear, old friends—already.

219 Action

Have you done something that makes you feel more vital or alive today? Have you done something for someone else to help that person feel good about living in his body or on the planet?

One politely opened door or a positive word about the right color tie are gestures of recognition. Common human courtesy is amazing and priceless.

JULIAN LYNN

220 Sweet Support

A gentle rain fell all day today. Rain washes the air we breathe and acts as sweet support for our body's linings and its protective embrace. Skin is actually the body's largest organ, hugging us while keeping us safe. Let it breathe.

221 Channel

The idea of a central, energetic column, running from the pelvic floor to the crown of the head and through the torso, exists in multiple Eastern traditions. Fill it consciously and daily with the luminosity you breathe in from the sunlight all around you. Radiate!

222 Seeing Double

My world view includes the gift of second sight. Thus, the world is made up of its incomparable physical beauty, which stands as a physical framework for its natural, spiritual Light. To paraphrase C.S. Lewis, you *are* the Spirit; you *have* a body. Thus, if I am fresh from meditation, I may be inclined to see your Light.

There are days when I wish each of us would be able to see the world through this lens—not to change the essence of who anybody is, in terms of identity, but to assist everyone in becoming free and open to the direct experience of the singular Light which connects us all and reveals the world's perfection.

In the atmosphere, there is a layer of Light created by selfless thoughts, kind wishes and heartfelt prayers—from every

JULIAN LYNN

place on the planet and regardless of religious affiliation. This layer is further strengthened and supported by what the Buddhists would term "right action."

Try holding space in and around your body to welcome this, your Light, back into its home. Strive to see that which is most luminescent in strangers and loved ones. Allow the demands of social definitions to fall away. In this way, it becomes easier to honor those you meet while working around human folly.

223 On Film

Mythologies in minds and hearts turn life into high tragedy, applaud-worthy comedy, drama or heart-warming adventure. Look at your life as a film director would. Categorize your life production, what are you filming?

YOGA'S DEVOTIONAL LIGHT

224 Explorations

Meditation (dhyana) provides us with chances to explore issues, relationships or circumstances, needing a greater depth of attention than everyday life affords. While in meditation, the natural opening of our consciousness produces a desire to dialogue with the "subject" (or "object") of our specific inquiry or focus.

Ideally, this dialogue is a request from one heart to another heart for an authentic conversation. And, when we attempt to connect in this way—with another soul—we must be careful to ask for permission *first*.

Meditation, as a practice, requires repeatedly that we think, feel and act from a seat of integrity. Life becomes clearer from this vantage point.

JULIAN LYNN

225 Road to Charity I

Leaving the hotel banquet area with a full pitcher of pristine tonic water and a tray of stemmed glassware, my friend George and I are headed back upstairs to meet with our writers' group.

"How do you rate?" I exclaim. "Free pitcher of tonic water for the whole crew? They made me pay for the pitcher I treated last week—not much—but, still." (It is straight complaint.)

"Yeeeaaaah," George's vowels are long with sweet tea, his hair is unruly and the corduroy jacket he wears has professorial leather patches on the elbows, "But, you *look* like you have money," he muses.

"But, you look like you have money." I consider his observation.

Clearly, George is not alone in his perspective. Whether it is a request for

YOGA'S DEVOTIONAL LIGHT

food money or fuel money, I am often approached to fulfill requests for charity.

    At some point, I decide that all of this wishful requesting is coming about as a result of my being white, female, middle-aged or of a certain demeanor. Or, perhaps it is more important that I am middle-aged, female, of a certain demeanor and white. I am unsure about which trait or combination thereof, in terms of my external social markers, makes me seem so very approachable. Nonetheless, many members of society, who are in need, perceive me to be a source of potential, emergency assistance.

    So, it happens that one day, while loading the back of my parked vehicle, next to two, deep-discount stores, I am approached yet again for cash. (I do not carry or offer cash assistance.) From behind me, I hear the cash request come in from a man looking for gas money, so he and his friends can finish their drive south to Phoenix, Arizona.

On this day, something in me snaps as I reach some unknown threshold. Also, I am hungry, which is always dangerous. And, I have my hand in a newly opened large bag of discounted corn chips.

Whipping around to meet my would-be recipient of charity, I turn so abruptly and ferociously on this unsuspecting Latino man that he puts both of his open hands in the air, while backing away from me very slowly and responding, "Whoa—lady—take it easy. Relax."

Pulling my hand from my bag of chips, I tell him I cannot offer him any gas money, but that I could give him and his friends my newly opened bag of precious corn chips. He graciously accepts my offer. I explain to him that I have just finished emptying my pockets at the local discount stores. And, we part ways in quiet peace.

YOGA'S DEVOTIONAL LIGHT

226 Real Words

The mouth, tongue and vocal organs are, potentially, a means by which we learn to express the desires of our most illustrious Perfection.

Impeccable speech, combined with right action, calls out to the awakening and awakened hearts of others.

227 Stepping Forth

Acts of faith can feel like a walk in the dark or a march down the gangplank. Yet, catching us each time is neither a night darkness nor a body-swallowing, cold sea of water, but the invisible arms of Divine Mother. Proceed with guided prudence and the aid of grounded friends.

JULIAN LYNN

228 The Glade

In reading Shankara again, we are met with those many aphorisms describing various states of Samadhi.

If we have not yet been to the glade in the middle of the forest, it feels like a mythical place far, far away; when, in fact, it is this very real place here, here and now. But, how do we get there?

Lie down on a blanket in the grass of your favorite park, where it is safe, and simply *BE*. Allow Divine Mother to lift the dust from your tired body and breathe in the sweet air that surrounds your holy frame. Tingle a little. And, when you are refreshed, share your sense of renewal with a simple gesture toward another appropriate, receptive person.

229 Focus

Single-pointed focus, keeping the mind focused on one thing for an extended period of time, sounds daunting—almost impossible. In this practice, we are asked to collect and consolidate observational powers and personal energy within and around ourselves.

Then, when we are in Stillness, we have the luxury of turning our fully focused attention and consolidated energy to the one task at hand. This type of focus assists us in maintaining alignment.

230 Fingers

Spread your fingers. Relax. Repeat.

JULIAN LYNN

231 Mind Passion

In the *Yoga Sutra*, there is a nod given to balancing our practice schedule with the recommendation to follow "inquiries of interest," aiding us in both gentling and strengthening the sometimes wild, yearning intellect and mind. This ancient permission slip, given to us by Patanjali himself, encourages us to embrace our unique, offbeat interests—guilt free.

When was the last time you visited the public library to check out five books, three films or six albums on a few pet passions, whether they be hiking in remote areas, the art of slow cooking, jazz music or the collecting and pressing of botanical samples? Go ahead, exercise your mind. Patanjali recommends it.

232 Motivations

The importance of purity of intension cannot be stressed enough. If we are committed to working on clarity of vision and toward the growth of a more luminescent, liberated heart, we must ensure that the major push behind our actions is service-based. Start small.

Sometimes the smallest act, from the pure kernel of a stranger's heart, makes the biggest ripple in a recipient's day.

233 Steady

Stand steady in the Self. Clarity in an interaction begins with full presence. Understanding comes in quiet Stillness.

234 Brahman

Returning to the beginning of Patanjali's *Yoga Sutra*, sincere and eager students of yoga are urgently reminded of the importance of surrendering to Brahman. Brahman is often translated as God. But, this translation, because of our various Western conceptualizations and personifications of God, causes discomfort for some yoga practitioners—whether they consider themselves theists, nontheists or fall somewhere in between. And, it does not really address the conceptualization of Divinity as it stands in some of India's philosophical traditions.

Thus, to what or to whom is Patanjali so urgently asking us to surrender?

235 Abiding

The Supreme Being, as Patanjali articulates, is a force that is all knowing, eternal, the ultimate teacher and One, who never behaves with misapprehension.

The wisdom of this Force is at work throughout all of Nature. It is the drive for life which tells the flowering bulb, which way to extend itself to the light of the sun, even when the bulb has been placed upside down in the ground by the hands of an inexperienced gardener or the hands of a small child.

236 Mercy

Offer up a few words of kindness.

JULIAN LYNN

237 Coming to Be

We are planted here, some of us, like the perennial bulbs in the garden of a novice or an inexperienced gardener—because some of our guardians or parents possessed less than optimal rearing skills, may have harbored pain from unrealized dreams or exhibited difficult emotional or lifestyle issues.

Yet, like the garden bulbs, seeking the nourishing sunlight, we have at the core of our very being this *knowing*, an untarnished force within the body, wanting not only to survive but to thrive, grow and bloom.

This force of knowing is uncovered and rediscovered during our dedicated practice of spiritually-grounded yoga.

YOGA'S DEVOTIONAL LIGHT

238 connecting

In a plant, the sacred growth force, that reaches for the sun when the first spring light comes and that sends roots into the earth when it warms, is the *What* and *Whom* we seek connection and conversation with during our asana, pranayama and meditation practices.

When we are consistently attentive during practice, this Force shows itself to be compassionate, forgiving and life-affirming, revealing to us how to want not only what is best for our singular Self, but also what is best for that which is Self in others as well.

Surrendering completely to this Wisdom buoys us up like a life preserver, when we become caught in life's rapids.

JULIAN LYNN

239 Delicacies

When a practitioner of sense withdrawal (pratyahara) reemerges into the world of sights, fragrances, sounds, textures and flavors and with a clean palate on every score, the tendency to act the part of excessive gourmand is gone. Sensory offerings are then carefully chosen and fully savored for the holy acts that they are. Awe returns to sensory living.

240 Chatter Box

Finding external balance requires internal listening. Curling the tongue, so that the tip of the tongue rests on the roof of the mouth, may assist in quieting a chattering mind. A mind at rest opens us to listen for our internal Voice.

241 Repair

In the late afternoon, most especially if something has not worked out, I remind myself that I am one person among a sea of billions of striving souls on the planet.

This is when I take a breath and, stepping into my changing room, reappear as the undercover, Faerie Godmother to do something kind for some unsuspecting fellow traveler on this plane of existence.

Try it. Pay off another person's library fines, ask to wash someone's car windshield at the gas station, collect flowers to give to a neighbor or pay an expiring parking meter—anonymously. Think small. Be creative.

You will begin to observe that hope is reborn, not in one heart, but in two.

JULIAN LYNN

242 Steadying

Holding ourselves steady in Samadhi is challenging as we move through the world, especially as the broken-hearted approach, that we often shift in and out of the experience. Let it happen.

Walk around a park, reseat yourself on your meditation cushion, take a break with your yoga mat and press forward with Union quietly renewed.

243 Freedom

Learn to give freely, so you may receive freely, trusting that the Divine is aware of your very individual needs. Dignity grows with this practice.

244 Road to Charity II

On the road to charity, an incident where I startled a gentleman, who was asking me for fuel money, proves pivotal to my new approach in answering a request for a handout or assistance.

But, first, I had to work through the shame I felt about my own response of anger at receiving yet another request for a fiscal handout. Although we have chosen to live a life of simplicity and frugality, no one else knows this. Given my appearance on nongardening days, it might be expected that people would approach me.

The second thing I realize is this: If we cannot turn to one another for help, to whom are we to turn? Everyone should retain the right to request assistance from another human being as long as they are not aggressive, offensive or overly intrusive.

JULIAN LYNN

The third thing this exchange teaches and which makes it stand out above many others is that I actually caused fear to rise in a fellow human being. On that day, I decided I did not want my being on the planet to cause someone else fear or a large degree of unnecessary discomfort.

Finally, I determine that I need to accept a role society is clearly asking me to play, that of minor relief provider. Internally, I have to ask, "Maybe this is a role Divine Mother would have me fulfill?"

To this end, I attempt to keep pop-top, canned goods, with plastic utensils attached, specifically for handing out. If someone is truly hungry, I make an offer of food from the space of a clean heart. When people are indeed hungry, this form of charity is usually gratefully received.

But the important questions are much larger: Who shapes us? Who tells us who we are as individuals? And, what if society attempts to thrust a role upon us that is far less than our individual best or perfect whole? What if society attempts to push us into a box that does not address our inherent Light or goodness? Consider these questions each time someone responds to you based solely on external appearances or social markers.

    We each have the ability to reject another's limiting conceptualizations. Are we being asked to fill a role greater than the one we thought we were designed for, or are we being limited by someone else's restrictive or outmoded ideas?

    In my case, I was and continue to be asked to fill roles greater than I ever conceived of playing. Thus, society has caused me to become more charitable, aware, compassionate and thoughtful. For this, I am grateful.

JULIAN LYNN

245 Considerations

There is one, very important sentence buried in B.K.S. Iyengar's *Light on Yoga*, which encourages hatha-yoga practitioners to dispense with select postures once a certain level of mastery has been attained.

This sentence encourages us, as committed yogis, to remain flexible in our approach to what we think of as a necessary routine. We are encouraged to listen to our bodies and allow for change.

There are circumstances under which our asana practice requires adjustments: fatigue, injury, pregnancy, giving birth, a change in season, physical maturation or anatomical singularities. As life moves forward, explore a range of options in the postures you visit and the sequencing you use. Remember, time, maturation and wisdom are close friends.

YOGA'S DEVOTIONAL LIGHT

246 The Gunas

The gunas, which may be referred to as qualities, traits or forces, are a system of classification used to describe the phenomenal world in Vedanta. The system may describe anything from activities to foods.

Rajas: Rajasic energy is passionate, swift, fiery, kinetic and of this world. It is a force which shakes, spins and moves.

Tamas: Tamasic energy is stagnant, slow and inert, feeling like it is fermenting.

Sattva: Sattvic energy is considered optimal because it is said to be in harmony with natural laws, purity and goodness.

The key thing to remember is that our search is for a personal definition about what is sattvic for us at a given moment in time. Learn to read the body.

JULIAN LYNN

247 Cast Flowers

In Shankara's wisdom, he reminds us, "The arrow which is shot at an object with the idea that it is a tiger, does not, when the object is perceived to be a cow, check itself, but pierces the object with full force." Because our perceptions are often incomplete and inaccurate, it is best to cast flowers—even at tigers.

248 Pure Core

If investing in our own reinvention, it must be for the purpose of listening for and heeding the altruistic desires within our own pure Being. Caring for the frame will follow.

249 Darshan

The weather has shifted, and the heat is milder and kinder for pedestrian travel. The whole of me is up and humming with gratitude and joy.

Rounding the corner on a block, where I do not normally walk, I pass three houses, when a toddler steps out from behind a parked vehicle in one of the driveways. His arms are waving wildly, as I pass. This is a holy gesture of formal recognition, a blessing of the highest order.

I want to bow to him, in a formal and dramatic way, in honor of the Rumi story that I know about darshan (the granting of a blessing).* But, we sparkling souls settle for reciprocal waves of enthusiasm over the gift of this day.

JULIAN LYNN

*On his way to work, the great Persian poet and Sufi mystic, Jalal ad-Din Rumi, is said to have bowed to each young child he met on his way. One day, after Rumi had already conferred blessings and been blessed by each child in his sight, a young boy was seen running across a neighboring field. The boy's arms were waving wildly as the boy ran, shouting and asking the Master to wait. Rumi waited. The boy arrived breathless and ready for darshan.

250 Letting Go

People often curb their own unfolding because conditional "love" and less-than-optimal living patterns feel normal.

Let go of the past and injurious behavioral patterns. It will be amazing.

251 Discernment

Mental clarity involves bringing our neutral Observer into each circumstance, individual relationship, place and time. We must suspend superficial, snap judgment, staying open to discern what is going on around us in the here and now. And, we must determine how, if at all, we are to become involved.

Keep the mind clear while running through a check list of immediate sensory and emotional experiences: What am I seeing? What am I hearing? What am I tasting? What am I smelling? What am I touching? How do I feel? This is how we learn to place our precious, vital energy—our Light—into the most appropriate circumstances and where it, as well as we are most needed.

JULIAN LYNN

252 Mirth

I am visiting a favorite out-of-town, health-food store. Near the specialty baked goods, I see a mature couple, also from out-of-town, trying to decide what to select from a wide range of dessert and deli items.

In an effort to help, I recommend the dairy-free, chocolate tofu "cheese" cake. It comes out that I am not actually a chocolate consumer anymore because, I explain, chocolate causes hiccups in the float trip of my consciousness. Thus, I choose to abstain.

"Like caffeine?" asks the man.

"Yes, like that," I answer.

"So, you prefer a smooth, even ride?"

"Yes, it is much finer, more reliable."

A few minutes and three aisles later, this comes over the intercom, "The sandwich for Stud Muffin is ready in the deli. The sandwich for Stud Muffin is ready in the deli for pick up."

I know it is my new friend and his wife, who are up to some silly fun. Age does have privileges. These are the unadvertised joys of yoga. Seek them.

253 In the River

The acceptance of life's highly varied and flavorful moments is contingent upon our ability to remain grounded and centered, while—with resilience—we allow life's experiences to wash over, pass around or flow through us.

The exception to this is when we feel called or choose to work for positive, social change which is in everyone's highest Light and may defy conventional norms. Then, we should paddle consciously and fiercely.

JULIAN LYNN

254 Open Heart

Sitting in single-pointed focus (dharana) allows us to sift through the space in and around the body to release antiquated patterns of thought, speech and action. Quite often we encounter uncomfortable memories arising as we face ways in which we have displayed disregard or unkindness toward others or toward ourselves in the past.

What then?

Forgive. Reextend compassion toward yourself and others. Then, forgive again. Sometimes, keeping forgiveness in our hearts means we stop seeing a person or revisiting a situation, choosing instead to move on.

In the widening space of a newly cleared heart, the Self may be fully received and grow bigger. Make room.

YOGA'S DEVOTIONAL LIGHT

255 Golden Mean

Classic texts stress a balanced approach to physical practice. Postures are about relaxing into a position, while listening for what is going on in the body. The conversation we have with the body is sometimes capable of saving us from unnecessary wear and tear. So, pick up the in-house phone, and allow your consciousness to patch you through.

256 Flight Path

There are geese flying overhead, and what a raucous conversation they are having. Birds are dear neighbors.

JULIAN LYNN

257 Mala

A set of prayer beads is one of the best tools to use in finding that sweet space of consistent gratitude.

Find a comfortable, seated position and rest your hands on your thighs. Take the mala in your dominant hand; set the mala across the middle finger after the first joint. The string of beads will come to the inside of the ring and small fingers. Start with the first bead after the strand's tassel. Use your free thumb to pull the beads toward you, one at a time. With each bead, name one thing for which you are grateful. (Traditionally, the right hand is used exclusively. Alternate hands every other day to balance the brain.)

Soon, you will note your resting mind automatically remembering to be thankful for life's exquisite details.

YOGA'S DEVOTIONAL LIGHT

258 conceit

    Standing at a rack of clothing, while sorting through second-hand items at a large bin in a resale store, I overhear a conversation between a cognitively disabled worker, a woman in her forties, and her manager-coworker, another woman who is perhaps in her mid-twenties.

    "Are you headed home after you finish that rack, Marguerite?" the manager intones, glancing back across her shoulder. The manager is clearly bright, fast and on the move, keeping everything and everyone in the store up and humming.

    "Yes," the disabled woman answers with a broad smile expanding across her face, "my puppies are waiting for me—for a walk and dinner." Her head tilts slightly to the left as her words drag out. Her

JULIAN LYNN

self-applied lipstick is gently defying her upper-lip line in a couple of places.

"How many puppies do you have, Marguerite?" the manager shoots back more out of politeness, it seems, than actual interest.

"Three," Marguerite responds with her smile growing even broader, as she glows even brighter, thinking about her canine companions waiting at home.

This is the point at which I have to stop my mindless sorting and face my shame. My second sight has kicked in.

When I look up from the clothing rack where I am standing to see and hear the last exchange, the sheer brilliance of Marguerite's spiritual space is stunning, radiant and a beautiful, holy purple—an unprecedented shade of deep violet, a color most associated with individuals on a committed spiritual path or with those in

YOGA'S DEVOTIONAL LIGHT

profound, Divine alignment. I know Marguerite to be one of God's chosen.

My shame is complete, displacing all other thoughts and emotions. Trained as a teacher, I automatically engaged in the act of assessing the speakers' cognitive abilities without even looking up. I was doing the normal, intellectual sorting teachers are trained to do, comparing the conversationalists, with the same attentiveness I had applied to pushing through garments on the rack. I was guilty of placing Marguerite and her manager into their respective "groups" for teaching or instructional purposes.

But, who is requiring assignment to a special class today? I am.

A person's spiritual state is not reflected by his intellectual prowess, social position or wit, nor is it even necessarily expressed when we extend seemingly appropriate words or gestures

JULIAN LYNN

toward a cause, group or person. The quality of one's spiritual state is best nurtured through quiet, life-affirming action, with compassion attached to it.

Thus, we must move our consciousness from the mind into the heart. This is where the sacred Self abides. It is in the context of the heart that we must plant and cultivate the seeds of innocence, sincerity and respect for the sanctity of All beings, creatures and Creation.

259 Rise & Shine

Every day we wake up and check the weather. What if we dedicated that time to checking in with the Self?

YOGA'S DEVOTIONAL LIGHT

260 Talk

We engage in an overextension and loss of personal energy any time we talk about business that is not our own. And, more often than not, we are creating stories of conjecture based on a few tawdry scraps of hearsay. Why not withdraw from this pattern of behavior?

There is strength, integrity and comfort in embracing people where they stand—within the Mystery.

261 Nature

Gratitude is felt for the late rains. Tiny snakes appear around the garden's edges. When we meet, we say, "Hello," and graciously go our separate ways.

JULIAN LYNN

262 Edges

Most of us have had a childhood experience where, through deep focus, all of our personal edges fall away. Pure perception is like this. Pure perception comes to us in living meditation, when we let go of memories, ideas and projections about the future, as well as current conceptions regarding other people and their situations, about whom or which we may actually know nothing.

If we are making an inquiry, for purposes of clarification, pure perception may reveal another person's previously hidden pain. If we perceive that we are receiving a glimpse into another person's emotional state, then, we are being asked to build a new heart on the cornerstone of compassion. To remain in this state, release judgment. Love will move in.

263 Creating Time

Once, my primary teacher in Pranic Work assigned me the task of doing five things for myself every day. At the time, I was an overwhelmed mother, wife and daughter—among the other roles I played.

I thought to myself, "She is crazy. How am I going to carve time out of my day for myself?"

Then, I discovered that in caring for myself I could actually *create* time for everything and everyone else.

264 Acceptance

We cannot find external acceptance, until we know internal acceptance.

JULIAN LYNN

Autumn

265 Easwaran

According to Vedanta, on our life journey, many of us bear a great deal of pain or blocks to joy, left over from previous adventures or incarnations and which may not lift from our consciousness with just a few meditative sittings.

We know we have things to work through when we open to feel joy and encounter grief instead. Grief, too, may be lifted and shifted out. Addressing grief, buried anger and other emotions takes fortitude, tenacity and commitment.

This process of release is worth every ounce of time put into it. It is worth hundreds of sittings. Universal compassion grants respite for the overly weary. Ask for help. Allow Love to abide. This is the nature of Brahman.

JULIAN LYNN

266 Clouds

The depth and quality of light in clouds is reminiscent of the depth and quality of Light, present in each Spirit.

Try Spirit gazing today. Approach each person as a unique cloud formation in the sky. Insights into the very nature of another person's Being may occur.

267 New Tools

The attitude of defiance, used as a tool of self-preservation within the context of a difficult or rocky childhood, must be consciously dismantled in adulthood to allow for the rediscovery of the sacred Self and the free flow of Grace.

268 Links

There are times, when in that perfect space of seamlessness, I am approached by the truly devout, wishing to share a profundity from a personal, spiritual experience. In that person's sharing, our hearts are linked and the initial wonder of a sacred moment spills forth from that person's heart and experience. Then, wishing to speak more freely, the individual asks after my external, social identity or my religious affiliation.

If conversation, on an external, social level, renders me a non-affiliated match, the speaker breaks the Universal Thread; and, both of our hearts suffer terribly.

Through the pain of our separation, I will remain in gratitude for our meeting and love You always.

JULIAN LYNN

269 Innocence

In meditation, we might find ourselves participating in a series of visitations to various planes of consciousness or memory. Visiting these places usually elicits a variety of emotional responses.

If a resulting planar visitation produces a cascade of less-than-optimal emotional experiences, sit with each situation or scenario, asking that each one be carefully and *consciously* resolved with the participation of your own highest Light and all those involved. This is the work and path to unhindered, yogic Union.

Moving through a burdensome load of past issues frees us to Love ourselves and others again, with a heart full of innocence and pure abandon.

YOGA'S DEVOTIONAL LIGHT

270 New Skin

Yoga assists us with the process of shedding our old skin by encouraging new habits. But, what do we do in the context of a new skin? How do our thoughts change, our words, our actions? Are we able to stop time for others and become more charitable, forgiving and patient?

This adaptation to a new life with tender skin is the greatest and most challenging work of all.

271 Late Night

Night comes early for the autumn gardener. Turning the earth, while the sun peers over my shoulder, I feel the coolness of autumn's breath on my back.

JULIAN LYNN

272 You Misread Me

Conversation circles about my head as I eat a meal among a large group of new acquaintances. I am sampling, for the first time, an ethnic cuisine from another region of the world.

About one-third of the way through the meal, I realize it would be a kindness to share this food with my husband who is at home, dog-sitting. Only half-attentive to the conversation going on around me, I begin thoughtfully dividing the food items on my plate, finishing only what my body requires and reserving the rest.

Still new to the community, my husband and I discover that, according to local perceptions, we live in a "less-than-optimal" neighborhood. The first time this observation was made, we had only been in our house a few days. A visiting

YOGA'S DEVOTIONAL LIGHT

plumber diplomatically asked us whether or not we were sure we had found the right place to live, further hinting that we might find "our community" in another neighborhood. Nonetheless, for me, and for us, the neighborhood we have selected has proven to be exactly right.

In our neighborhood, we have a large, fenced backyard surrounded by natural lawns, a real plus when you enjoy organic gardening and the company of two active dogs, who love to eat grass and chase balls.

Because we prefer to walk (or I ride my bicycle), we are in the best quadrant of the city for both lighter traffic and biking convenience, as well as walkable food stores. In our neighborhood's initial configuration, our neighborhood echoed the positive experiences we had in graduate-school housing, living among people of a myriad of cultures.

JULIAN LYNN

Because my husband loves picking up snippets of foreign languages, he shouts good day in Romanian to our gardening neighbor to the west of our yard, who brings us mounds of fresh produce and eggs. We receive garden-fresh Asian squash from neighbors on either side.

But, tonight, my dining companions, who are from different neighborhoods, ventured out to experience things in an area of urban renewal, closer to my home.

As the meal progresses, unfinished plates of food are pushed away with leftovers to throw out. I think of the verse from the *Taittiriya Upanishad*, reminding us to waste not food, water or fire, which echoes my family's love of economy. A few members from the party ask for take-home containers. The server brings large boxes to our table. (This restaurant has made an effort to stock sustainable, pressed-paper containers.)

YOGA'S DEVOTIONAL LIGHT

Assessing my own food gift, I decide to pack everything easily into my extra-large, unsullied napkin. "Why waste the life of another tree?" I reason. The neatly wrapped parcel slides easily into my handbag. When I bob up, I catch a few looks—maybe. Looks or not, what I can tell you is this, "*You misread me.*"

I am not what you think I am; I like to share—especially precious, sacred food. This is an act of respect for All life.

273 Trek

In all fairness, the trek from reactive personality to universal heart can be long and challenging. Clinging to and nursing old pleasures and pains, we allow them to become identity even while the pure, radiant nugget of Grace, an oasis of Peace, sits as an open lotus in our hearts.

JULIAN LYNN

274 Jnana Yoga

Jnana yoga, which is sometimes referred to as the path of wisdom, traditionally relies on studying the rich and broad scriptural works available in Sanatana Dharma, The Eternal Way or Law, as the people of India refer to Hinduism. (Of yoga's many traditional methods for approaching Union, it should be noted that hatha yoga is sometimes considered the least refined.)

And, yet, the beauty of practicing hatha yoga is that we may choose to draw scriptural support, not only from Vedic tradition, but from the sacred texts of our personal, religious heritage as well. Asana, pranayama and meditation, no matter what life-affirming literature we choose, assist us in organizing consciousness and opening a sincere and aspiring heart.

275 Comprehension

If we set external identities aside, what would we communicate? In most cases, after needs have been met, what we want is a compassionate ear, after the world has been overly harsh or when we seek forgiveness for the times we have stepped away from our integrity.

I hear you. It happened. Make amends. Forgive. Return to the Self.

276 New Routine

Change a routine to fluff the worn patterning of your mind. Take the scenic road home, visit a children's museum, smile and begin daydreaming anew.

JULIAN LYNN

277 Mirrors

The ego exists in a hall of mirrors. In exploring the issue of taking time to honor the internal child to promote healing, as well as making the permanent move into the heart, questions arise: When is the act of honoring the internal child, encouraging a genuine promotion of healing? Or, when does honoring the internal child devolve into overindulgence and the nursing of yet another old, emotional injury?

Returning to our mat practice or meditation cushion, visiting a dear friend, who is also on the path, and relying on critical, internal investigation become essential tools to opening the door on long-term well-being and emotional healing. Ask, listen, act and, then, trust your current, working truth.

278 Worn Shoes

Life offers us opportunities to explore many experiential planes—physical, creative, emotional, fiscal, intellectual, domestic and spiritual. Community grants us, as metaphorical travelers, the ability to map our plans and experiences in relationship to one another and the Self.

Life is enriched when we seek out experienced, companion travelers. Look for worn shoes. Talk to the wearer.

279 Grace Notes

Grace notes are often treated as embellishments. Yet, they define an entire era musically. That which is sacred is not an embellishment. Grace is woven into each detail of every melodic day.

JULIAN LYNN

280 Elements of Life

Sitting outside of the grocery store in my vehicle, collecting myself after moving through a crowd of frenetic shoppers, I look up from balancing my bank account to see a young girl riding in a shopping cart, held steady by one of her parents. She is about four. Her tongue is out as far as it can go. She faces the wind, checking the air with her tongue.

And, I think, "That's just it. As adults, we have forgotten how to explore the world with all of our senses—how to taste the world's freshness."

Be present to the Earth, her elements and your body this week—with all of your senses. Whenever you have a chance, take time to taste the wind.

281 Walking Path

The spiritual path is neither a linear walk nor a vertical climb but a thoughtful, meandering trail. Whether or not we are "on the path" is contingent upon the choices we make on a moment-by-moment basis. Thus, we choose to enter or remain on the path in each moment.

The critical life choices have to do with care and respect. How respectfully can we become hosts to our own Atman? How thoughtfully and inclusively can we behave toward Atman in our neighbors? In fellow creatures? How compassionate can we become? Generous? Merciful? Forgiving?

The ability to listen and respond accordingly, to whatever nudges, urgings or guidance may be provided, grows when we begin to operate more consistently from the Light nestled deep within our

JULIAN LYNN

hearts, while moving away from our personal, individual story and possibly selfish concerns.

So, for today, practice listening and responding to the world from the seat of Peace in your heart—your Universal Being.

282 Asana

Hatha yoga is designed to develop flexibility, not merely to support those already physically pliable. Likewise, it is designed to strengthen us, allowing those already strong to explore balance.

When entering into the sacred practice, do not apologize for where you find yourself; know that you are becoming who you were meant to be.

283 Histories

In our most intimate relationships, we often hold a myriad of limiting, inaccurate, yet defining stories and histories about others and our individual relationships with them. Events and stories about circumstances, more often than not, keep us and other "players" in a state of behavioral and role stasis.

Who could or would we become if we released limiting stories and histories, allowing each other to unfold? Moving into silence and remaining open to the questions: Who am I? And, how might I serve the Self within me and others, so we can grow and unfold?—sometimes results in amazing changes and the complete redefinition of roles in relationships among willing life-partners and companions.

JULIAN LYNN

284 Inside

Stop searching for the external guru. Stop trying to thread the strings of your heart through someone else's essence. You are already whole.

Shankara reminds us how imperative it is to touch this Reality in our own right, "The true nature of things is to be known *personally*...and not through a sage; what the moon exactly is, is to be known through one's own eyes..." The Observer is inside. The Teacher is already inside. Wholeness you are already.

285 Flower

In the garden of my heart, I planted a flower for you. Please tend to me as you would a delicate bloom.

286 Guidance

"Do you teach intuition?" a man asks me at a table, where my books are on sale.

"Do I teach intuition?" I ask the question again. "I do not think someone can 'teach' intuition. When the Self, or someone's Light, is grounded and centered in the body, a person usually knows how to proceed in a given situation.

"And, when we express a sincere desire to walk a path of service, then intuitive nudges or Divine guidance generally come through with greater accuracy and frequency, aiding us in that service.

"Thus, in my experience, intuition is not taught, but Divine guidance may be granted to us, when we are ready."

JULIAN LYNN

287 Orchestra

Each of us possesses a rhythm and instrument uniquely our own. In a group class, during a solo, physical practice or in meditation, we sometimes encounter our personal rhythm and instrument in heightened ways.

A cellist's music may be enjoyed in solo performance or in the context of an orchestra. Whether we experience our rhythm and instrument in solo or concert, we should come to appreciate our singular place in the grand scheme of things.

288 Canopy

Skating across fall's acorns, I have walked across the treetops of giants.

289 It's God's Party

Late one Saturday afternoon, having finished my errands on my bicycle, I approach a favorite location of quiet contemplation and meditation. It is adjacent to a Roman Catholic Church, where a beautiful white, marble statue of Divine Mother stands behind a fountain in a small garden setting.

Sometimes, I stop to sit and collect myself at this location, or realign to ensure that my highest Light is grounded and centered in my body before moving on. Traveling as I prefer to do, by bike or on foot, gives me enough time to remain in that space of devotion, so that I may respond to the meditative leadings that guide me through my best days.

There are times when I simply walk or bike past this place. But today, after

JULIAN LYNN

locking my bicycle, I receive a clear nudge to enter the church, where a Saturday Mass is already in progress.

The church is amazingly bright inside, painted light blue with white accents and statuary. An immense amount of light from the late afternoon sun streams into the sanctuary through long, stained glass windows. Two firmly strumming guitars join everyone together to form the musical heart of the Mass, as one elderly, clearly limping priest leads us through the forms of worship. The service atmosphere is one of gracious ease. This elderly man seems comfortable, as though he has served these people for a very long time.

As the priest makes his way rather painfully up the few steps to the pulpit to deliver the homily, he nods his head, saying, "You may be seated."

(In way of full disclosure, I should mention that I was raised in a service-oriented, Protestant church, with one cross as our only piece of iconography.)

The priest opens his homily with a very informal tone and personal story, "I was in my study the other day, when I looked up to see the baby Jesus, and we had a moment there—Jesus and I—a quiet moment of Peace."

He has no notes and is speaking in a comfortingly direct tone from a sincere heart. "There is Jesus, God—the Father, Mother Mary, Saint Joseph and a whole complement of Holy Saints." His tone becomes more official, "So, *get there*. Find someone you feel comfortable praying to, and get to that place of Peace." He clears his throat before proceeding, while adjusting his weight on his legs.

"Oh, yes. The reading. The prodigal son.* A difficult reading for some. Well, in short, it's God's party.

*Christian *Bible*, Luke 15:11-32

JULIAN LYNN

"You know, I was ordained over fifty years ago, and my parents were so excited that they wanted to throw a big party—rented the local VFW hall.

"Most of you know, I am from a small, farming community. Everyone knew everyone else. So, there were going to be people at that party in their best bib overalls and some in ties and suit coats.

"The Millers, Baptists, asked my folks about giving me an appropriate gift. They wanted to give me a necktie. My parents told them I would never wear a necktie. (He pulls gently on his clerical collar.) But, they were welcome to come to the party, and no gift was necessary.

"Everyone came. *Everyone* came to wish me well. There were neighbors—Methodists, Baptists, a few Lutherans and our people (Catholics).

"And, of course the Millers, good upstanding Christian people that they were, brought me a gift box with a necktie. So, you see, it is God's party. Remember that. Look around to your neighbors. Everyone is invited.

"So, after the party, I sent the Millers a thank-you for the tie because they were doing what was right for them, celebrating in their way. The gift was respectful. And, of course, Mr. Hanson came in his best, pressed overalls, because it was his way of showing respect.

"Now, I have been serving for over fifty years and have had one trip to Rome—a few years back now. Do you know what I saw? (He gestures with his hand bouncing below shoulder height.) Little, tiny nuns from Asia, Southeast Asia. They were everywhere. And, of course, our South-American brothers and sisters. Do you know what Rome actually smells like in the Vatican? It smells like—what's that yellow spice called?"

JULIAN LYNN

"Curry," a parishioner pipes up from one of the full pews.

"Yes, curry! Rome smells like curry," he exclaims. (Curried foods are not a regular menu item in this region.) "Yet, we are all neighbors; we are all family. So, ask after your neighbors' health, their children, their parents, even if they don't look like you. Love your neighbors. Love your family. Be respectful.

"And, remember, it's God's party. Oh, and pray for me, if you think of it. I have surgery on my other hip soon."

290 Playing

Sunlight plays across a neighbor's wooden fence. The black walnut's long, craggy arms bob in shadowy relief, craving Union with the blue sky.

291 Worth

Because my relationship with Atman was forged through my asana practice, the shift to teaching hatha yoga publicly caused me to experience a sense of loss around this once very private relationship.

Then, students began telling me they could only get to sleep on certain nights if they replayed, in their minds, the yoga-nidra practices we had done in class. This news was balm for my Spirit. Serve.

292 Crazed

Why the frenzy around yoga? Whatever your affiliation, tradition or school—it works. If it is not working, change the approach, teacher or location.

JULIAN LYNN

293 Vessel

In hatha yoga, where the approach to Samadhi involves attention to our physical practice, we need to remember we are being invited to render our vessel more balanced, comfortable, healthy and a joyful place for the Atman to reside.

Because of some cultures' focus on external appearances, modern yogis sometimes forget shared, community practice is not about attire, a body's proportions in relationship to another's or how we "perform" physically on the mat.

Asana practice is personal, intimate and *sometimes* done in group settings. Ultimately, though, the practice of asana's physical postures is designed to strengthen us for entrainment with our own Divinity.

294 Voice

Searching for our authentic voice, the voice of the Self, involves pushing against the extremes of our vocal register. When we are centered, we may even be asked to communicate things we would not typically consider speaking about.

Accept this new voice, even as it cracks. This is how to search for the true range of expression of your singular Light.

295 Back to Basics

Let yoga do its thing, and anxieties, tensions and false hopes will fall away when the body, mind and Spirit are brought back into balance and alignment. Sprinkle practices liberally throughout your week. Peace to you.

JULIAN LYNN

296 well-being

The concept of well-being relies on the assumption that we want what is best for ourselves. Yet, what keeps us from establishing healthy living patterns?

Sometimes it is a matter of education—you must know what to do to do it better. At other times, we refrain from appropriate self-care because we are damaging ourselves in an attempt to wrestle control from those who have damaged us in the past. (This is an amazingly common pattern.) And, there are other reasons for defiance. Yet, it is through our dedicated practice that we establish the internal dialogue leading to healthier patterns of living, improved self-care and liberation from the past.

297 Karma Yoga

The heart opens naturally under the bright sun of a dedicated practice. How do we work with the unbound joy we find developing in our hearts? If we carry unresolved pain from childhood or from broken relationships in adulthood, that first Light will mend those injuries.

Then, with the heart's mending underway, we are able to turn our attentions to broader concerns—that of service to the Self in others.

298 Split Ends

A heart divided does more damage than external issues. Unify the heart.

JULIAN LYNN

299 Touching Home

  Catching a yoga-inspired class at a health club, I notice a giant of a man with a chiseled body and an armband tattoo, featuring a distinctively Pacific-Islands cultural design, running around an equally chiseled and massive bicep.

  After class, I approach him, asking, "Is that a Maori tattoo on your arm?"

  He smiles broadly, answering, "No. But, close. I am Samoan."

  Well, tālofa and fa'afetai!" I offer him a formal greeting and thank-you in Samoan. His smile broadens further, as I continue, "Welcome to the Middle of Nowhere. How are you faring here?" His girlfriend has rolled up her yoga mat and now stands at his side.

  "A little homesick... My family is in L.A., but, I am finding a Samoan tucked

YOGA'S DEVOTIONAL LIGHT

here and there. So, I am not too lonely, and I can always fly home."

He is a gentleman. He humors me as I run through my short list of seven Samoan vocabulary words, which I learned from a friend, who once served two tours of duty with the Peace Corps on the islands.

We say farewells. Both of our Spirits are strengthened by the brief exchange.

300 Kiss

There is a lot of mundane in one human life, making it difficult to touch the extraordinary. But, touch the Extraordinary and that is all we want — pristine headwaters, perfect weather, pure air and unlimited sky.

When Reality comes to kiss us, nothing else compares, until we open again and begin to see that Reality is everywhere.

JULIAN LYNN

301 Chakras

Chakras are energetic centers positioned throughout the body's torso, neck and head. They both take-in and exhaust energy from interactions, transactions and practices. Chakras interface with the nadis in processing prana. B.K.S. Iyengar indicates there are seven primary chakras and four minor.

Try building an asana practice around the balancing of each major center, one center for each day of the week.

302 Real Yoga

Yoga asks us to come into Stillness, amid a holiday, grocery line of stressed and otherwise overwrought people.

303 Choices

As adults, we have the incredible luxury of being able to choose the social forms and traditions we would like to observe and honor. With the opening and expansion of our hearts, concerns usually become broader in scope than receiving another, new pair of shoes or the purchase of a few specialty items.

Families vary incredibly in how they receive news about shifting perspectives on holiday traditions. Thus, should you choose to announce new ideas and a desire for a shift in tradition, tread gently on the feelings of your immediate and extended families, remembering that olive branches open more hearts to the idea of lasting changes than abrupt words or sharp turns.

JULIAN LYNN

304 Raja Yoga

Hatha yoga prepares the body to sit for raja yoga, where meditation is the road to Union. With body awareness and core strength established, we may turn to training our singular mind. Approach this door of awakening without expectation. Hold patience in the heart and emotional tenderness for the expanding mind, as it is retrained. The red carpet will unfurl.

305 Disconnected

Violence, betrayals, lies and expressions of greed are acts engaged in by the injured in a state of profound misalignment. Peace comes, when we address *internal alignment first*, ironing out our personal inconsistencies, wrinkles and kinks.

306 Bus Stop

"Can you read this bus schedule?" a woman asks me, as I pass a bus shelter on my walk home from the library.

Stopping to help, I bend to squint in the low light of evening at the impossibly small print. The only light filtering in is from a dim street lamp.

"No," I answer. "I can't make it out at all. Where do you need to go?"

We have a brief conversation about her destination over the two rolling suitcases she has next to her. A nondescript handbag, in basic black, rests upon the larger piece of luggage as we talk.

"I need to get to the House of Refuge's pickup point in the next two hours. I'm in from L.A. I lost my job," she reports matter-of-factly. "The past two days have been awful. There was no fresh food

JULIAN LYNN

or fruit or juice or—*anything* like that to eat at the shelter for the past two mornings," she repeats herself. "It's all pancakes, biscuits and bread. I know it's awful to complain. Being homeless really sucks. Have you ever been homeless?"

"No," I answer. "We have been really fortunate. I think the bus you want may not stop here. I think it stops a block-and-a-half from here, just around the corner. Your pickup point is only six long blocks from that location. Do you want to walk? It is safe. I could walk with you," I offer her this option.

"No. I am all in. I was in a car accident, and my whole left side is a mess. I walked all over today," she explains. Her grey hair moves across her face with a gust of warm, night wind.

"You know, I called my mother to try and stay with her when I returned, and she wouldn't even let me stay two or three nights. Isn't that just sad, when your own mother rejects you?" she continues.

"Do you want me to roll your suitcases to the other stop for you?" I suggest, not wanting to abandon her.

She wonders, "Maybe if I just wait here. I can ride the bus around the loop and get to the pickup point in time? The bus comes every half-hour, right?"

"I think so, but I am not sure the bus you want stops here, though I am no expert on the local bus schedule or the routes even," I offer tentatively.

"Well, okay," she sighs with resignation, grabbing her purse to swing it onto her shoulder with her good arm. She talks all of the while, as I grab the two remaining, rolling suitcases and follow her, allowing her to set the walking pace.

"I used to work at the Children's Amusement Center here—years ago, when

I still lived in the area, before going out to L.A. It was so much fun—the activities, the families...the laughter. I'd like to do that again. Do you think that they will take me back with my injuries?

"I don't like being disabled. There's no dignity. People really don't treat you with any respect."

We crawl along, walking very slowly. I realize why the bus ride was preferable. The pace she has set is about one-quarter of my own. Just then a city bus goes by, *the* city bus, the one she needed. I see her whole body respond in one large crumpled, slumping gesture ahead of me.

"I am so sorry," I offer from behind her, while thinking to myself, "Why did I interfere in her evening?"

"Oh, it's okay. The trip will be shorter from the next stop," she offers me verbal absolution as we continue walking slowly down the block. She continues talking

YOGA'S DEVOTIONAL LIGHT

about her recent experiences as I observe the difficulties with which her body ambulates down the sidewalk.

"I am tired of not having anything positive to look forward to—not having any *fun*. Nothing has been *fun* lately. I am going to get a job so that I can have *fun* again." The resolve in her voice is pronounced, determined.

And, I pray, "God, please do not let this woman down."

Finally, reaching the second bus stop, I roll her two suitcases next to one another, leaving the handles extended.

"I'm sorry about the other bus," I issue another formal, verbal apology, knowing now how difficult the simple act of walking is for her.

"Oh, it's okay. I'll be okay. *I'm getting a job*. I can't live like this," she declares to me and herself.

JULIAN LYNN

"You take care," I respond in parting, turning to walk home. Half a block away, I remember the loose bits of change in my pocket, which I rescued from the road on my walk to the library. Pivoting swiftly, I run back to thrust the insignificant change into her good hand.

"Here. I'm sorry this is all that I have. It's not even bus fare."

"Thank you," she accepts the collection of coins politely. "Thank you for walking with me."

We part company. I am richer for the exchange and have moved into gratitude.

307 Social Fabric

In support of all socially engaged hearts...One fabric, many threads.

YOGA'S DEVOTIONAL LIGHT

308 community

In moving from the seat of our meditation cushion to function in society, it is challenging to maintain perspective on how to operate from the seat of our inherent goodness, especially when other peoples' ethical challenges push upon us.

Yoga's physical, asana component, when performed in a supportive, group setting, gives us an opportunity to practice holding our Light safely in the context of an active, moving body. We are able to rehearse holding the Self in a sea of similarly committed individuals.

In such settings, others—who are seeking reflection, restoration and grounding in true center—support our walk forward in strength and dignity.

JULIAN LYNN

309 Limitless

It is in patience we need to listen, and it is in possessing patience we may have the most difficulty. Fear causes us not to follow through, preferring instead the clatter and clamor of our own limiting beliefs or society's prescribed restrictions.

Yet, our pure Light is available and prepared to drive our actions in the directions required to aid and mend us; and, eventually, we may be able to provide a healing presence to those around us.

310 Prana

Prana is that which nourishes us, supporting us as we work on making positive life changes.

311 Glorious

At a program I attended, a man contemplated aloud about "things on the other side" of death. Resources he had read, talked about things being like they are here—only better. He wondered how it would work out because he had had the privilege of knowing two profound, intimate and primary relationships.

I sat quietly, while others spoke, wanting to reassure him, "In the end, we are orbs of Light, beyond our earthly roles and limitations. When we come together again, it will be to shine for one another, without the confusion of our earthly constraints, relationships or roles."

Shine for yourself and others today from that Universal place of Being.

JULIAN LYNN

312 The Flood

In virtually every origin story of the world's religious traditions, there is The Flood, where the righteous are saved by Divine intervention. Think of this story as allegory. As we practice, we are asked to wash away all that is not of our essence. Drawing closer to center and the Self, the Divine hand extends an olive branch of Peace to us. Dry land is nigh.

313 Inquiries

Stopping to ask after a person's health, her family members or interests is one of the most holy acts possible.

Listening is one the most generous gifts we can bestow on another.

314 The Movies

Dreamless sleep is one of the most restorative states for the body to experience. Yet, there are times when we have dreams—fanciful, imaginative, wild, discomforting or reassuring.

In having a memorable dream, first consider whether or not the dream is of any significance. (Some dreams are as Dickens' character Scrooge noted, "Just a bit of indigestion.") If you feel the dream is of importance, consider the dream's major themes. Before lying down to sleep the next evening, request another dream to help clarify the first.

Dream time is sometimes the only narrow path open to the obscured recesses of our hearts, where we have blocked our own sacred flowering of the Self.

JULIAN LYNN

315 Reality

Sustaining an experience of Union allows the ever-present ember in the heart to glow anew. Emotions of compassion, love, forgiveness, unbound joy and generosity well up. This is *IT.*

Tending a nascent, internal fire, set deep inside, is vigilant, demanding work— most especially as we move to take our candle's Light out and into the blustery and unpredictable weather of living.

316 Found

Capture the words inside of you, through an introspective asana practice, and find the life themes needing care.

YOGA'S DEVOTIONAL LIGHT

317 'Tis the Season

Coming into the holiday season there is a contagious excitement we feel when stepping into various contexts of community-at-large. Being encircled by a group of expanding hearts causes our own heart to lurch forward in expansion. Why not live with an expanded heart? Why not live that way all year around?

Plan on riding the group wave now. Then, after the holidays, rummage through your belongings to keep the excitement alive, and keep giving.

There is neither one season for giving nor is there one season for nourishing the natural generosity residing inside of you— year-round and always.

The holiday parties are on!

JULIAN LYNN

318 Eternity

It is the last day of a trip, visiting old haunts and dear friends. I have one final tea scheduled across town and over the mountain. Walking to catch the bus, I see its blue, backside pull away from a stop three blocks ahead of me.

"Too late," my body slumps in disappointment. "I must be meant to walk," I think, while lengthening and straightening my body for the hike.

Reorienting to determine the most time efficient path to the northwest side of town, I resume my brisk pace with the sun rising steadily overhead.

Savoring the details along the ascent, I try to remember the paths and trails I used over six years ago to cross this very terrain. I see runners pass, neighbors talk and dog walkers nod as I proceed gratefully across a section of relatively flat plateau. I am covering ground.

Finally, behind the last coffee shop on the way out of town, I turn my feet and my body sideways for the final descent down a steep slope and footpath of gravel and rocks, skidding down a few well-worn parts of the narrow trail.

"I am really late," I think to myself.

Walking into the roadside coffee shop, I announce the obvious to my patient and long-waiting friend, "I am late. I am so sorry, but I missed the bus. Thank you for waiting for such a long time for me."

She smiles as she folds her local weekly newspaper into quarters, "I have no concept of time." And, then, lifting her wrists, "I didn't even wear a watch."

After ordering tea, we sit back down. Four months of spiritual reading and experiences of the heart are to be covered. A holy curtain is drawn around our table

JULIAN LYNN

while time works its magic by standing completely still.

"This is Eternity," my friend stops to announce emphatically and mid-conversation. Then, she makes the statement again and with more conviction, "As far as I am concerned, this-is-IT."

I pause to consider life from that perspective. This-is-IT.

On my way home, I keep revisiting that one concept—that one emphatic statement, gifted to me by my spiritual friend. I begin using the idea to look more carefully at the activities in my life, through that singular prism.

And, I ask myself, "If this is indeed *Eternity*, would I really choose to be doing this or to continue doing that?"

And, I admit that some things, which I never thought would change, begin to give way to new and better possibilities.

319 Child

Attending to the voice of the Self, with as much attention as we employ in tending to the needs of our children, fosters in us the ability to become patient, forgiving and able to pick up our own broken pieces, when things happen in ways other-than-planned.

When we are practiced in listening, we can then turn to extend compassion to the hearts of those around us.

320 Flurries

Holidays are upon us. Slow down and revel in the mad rush of pulsating energy going on around you. Soak up as much of the good stuff as you can. Then, sit for a minute, and marinate in Stillness.

JULIAN LYNN

321 A Rich Life

Among those who possess material comforts, I hear conversations about good and charitable deeds done for those less materially fortunate. At times, these conversations become almost painful because some of these charitable people work on an unspoken assumption that, because their lives are materially comfortable or enhanced, other aspects of their lives—intellectual, emotional, domestic, spiritual—must also be fuller or richer. In this line of thinking there is a conceit and a spiritual poverty of material self-importance.

The assumption, articulated, sounds something like this: My materially generous Spirit is worth more than your materially struggling Spirit in the grand scheme of things. Things simply are not that way. External or material things or circumstances do not change our essential, individual worth or wholeness.

Wealth, poverty, generosity or parsimony would best be measured in kindnesses. The kindnesses we extend, share and receive—from the space of our unfettered hearts—are the things that make us and our lives rich.

322 Diwali

The lengthening hours of night invite us to turn again toward our internal flame. We are able to stoke the heart's deeper, eternal flame with renewed focus during our meditations. This is an act worthy of a grand celebration.

JULIAN LYNN

323 Fixed Notions

S[h]raddha, often translated as faith, actually encompasses the entire matrix of beliefs shaping our worldview, thereby impacting how we react, act and may choose to function proactively in our lives.

What happens when we hold the door open on our existing fixed ideas to allow the sunlight of change and new experiences into the corners of our unsorted, somewhat cluttered and often conflicting and contradictory store of beliefs? (And, there is usually a treasure trove of unbelievable material buried in the unexplored, unsorted heart.)

A well-tended heart is filled with a simple, unadulterated joy with Being. Joy comes through naturally. Allow it.

324 Spaciousness

    Many spiritual traditions hold forth the hope that an aspirant will enjoy a clear, open mind—free from preexisting impressions. Into this spacious and receptive mind and uncluttered consciousness, there is room enough to listen for the quiet voice of the Self in one's own heart or to answer the sound of another's heart calling out in need.

    Emptying ourselves to become free from our imagined priorities makes room for our ability to answer a greater set of needs, wishes and concerns. When we open in meditation and, then, faithfully answer these calls, the process creates days of enduring wonder, gratitude, joy, connection and Union.

JULIAN LYNN

325 Nadis

The nadis are a system of channels through which prana is said to flow, as well as nourish every cell in the human body. In classical texts, there is a network of 72,000 such channels, with three channels being primary.

The first two channels may be described as archetypically feminine and masculine along with parallel attributes. They cross back and forth through the body's main energetic centers (chakras). And, unless they are in an exceptional state of balance, we tend to feel slightly out of sorts as we bounce back and forth, metaphorically speaking, between two polarities and what they represent.

Think of bouncing between these two channels as akin to living in your lower brain stem, where your life choices are essentially flight, fight or freeze.

The third channel runs from the pelvic floor to the crown of the head, in front of the spine and behind the sternum. It is a column of light. When we move into the channel of this column, we have the opportunity to experience Peace. Living from this space, we have a myriad of conscious choices and may choose to come into compassionate Being.

326 Quality

After basic needs have been met, it is the quality of our interactions which determine the quality of our lives. Are you in your integrity? Peaceably walking your truth? Practicing your innate kindness, patience and natural generosity? Open.

JULIAN LYNN

327 Taste

Ayurveda breaks digestion down into three components: How we experience food in the mouth; how well the belly is able to digest what we have eaten; and, how our food choices "feed"—or provide prana throughout—the body. (Are we satisfied and nourished on all levels?)

Try applying this paradigm to activities. Activities should nourish, like food, leaving an exceptional aftertaste.

328 Thanksgiving

Whether celebrating bounty in a group or finding ourselves going solo, gratitude is fostered, found and captured in life's details. Find your mala and name one-hundred-eight things that cause joy.

329 Mind to Heart

It was through a practice from another spiritual tradition that I came to appreciate the fine line between Patanjali's single-pointed focus (dharana) and what T.K.V. Desikachar terms meditative "understanding of the object" (dhyana).

Select one experience of great discomfort in your life and the individual you perceive may have contributed to that discomfort. Hold that person and experience, as well as the prevailing emotion, at the center of the brow. Then, with everything in sharp focus in your consciousness, shift into the space of your compassionate heart.

In the compassionate heart, new understanding will be born, because this is where unconditional Love abides.

JULIAN LYNN

330 Talent

It seems that virtually every long-term relationship, whether that relationship is between two people, a person and a group or two organizations, can begin to suffer from the "malaise" of intimacy. If or when, the malaise sets in, it causes both parties to forget how incredible we, as individuals, are and how singular our gifts and talents can truly be. In any relationship, the rekindling of a sense of freshness, wonder and gratitude presents a significant challenge.

So, in case you have forgotten, you are whole and gifted. Practice and share your talents generously. We need you. And, we need the singular offering of your talents.

331 Evening

Before retiring for the evening, take a moment to recline on the floor in a place of safety and quiet. If you have lower back issues, roll a small, hand towel and place it comfortably under the small of your back. Close both of your eyes and exhale deeply and thoroughly. Then, inhale comfortably, evening your breathing pattern until the abdomen rises with each inhale and falls with each exhale.

Bring your legs together and point your toes until the tops of your feet feel like they are being stretched. If you have no shoulder injuries, on the next inhaling breath, extend your arms straight over your head, clasping your hands together, with the index fingers extended.

Stretch long and tall. Relax. Repeat.

JULIAN LYNN

332 Duality

Birth, death. Female, male. Young, old. Sweet, sour. Soft, hard. Wealth, poverty. Solo, together. To move beyond duality, we willingly address the fractures in our own rhythm, priorities, calendar, activities and practices.

The move beyond duality is a matter of wrapping ourselves in life's Mystery, as we seek nothing but our own unified consciousness and internal alignment.

333 Wabi Sabi

Meditation is a *practice*, where we discover something new about ourselves each time. Release the idea of perfection.

334 Old & Naked

A young, male internist reaches the door of my friend's room moments before I do, ushering himself across the threshold in one broad, brusque motion. Rounds. Thus, I defer to his sailing white coat, taking the chair outside of my friend's room to wait my turn. I am in the hallway of an extensive hospital complex.

The corridor feels hot and stuffy. Leaning my head back against the wall, I close my eyes. I cannot help but hear the conversation filtering out through the half-open door into the stale air.

Full of hurried efficiency, several comments are made to "the patient" about medical notes on his chart and with regard to his history. My elderly friend responds in an even, educated and

JULIAN LYNN

amazingly jocular tone, relating further pointed medical details that might be of interest to the young, virile student.

Despite being very sick, my friend retains his eloquence and sense of humor. I smile inside with admiration on behalf of my friend. Bravery. Humanity. Decency.

The internist, however, is all business and is not biting—a dead fish. Specimens. Dissections. Cadavers. Diseases. Science. Pathology. The white coat is not even nibbling at the conversational bait of warm humanity cast before him.

I sense my friend is suffering at this lack of basic human recognition. One warm, live human being, albeit sick, would like to talk with the other warm, live human being, come on rounds.

"Hel-lo-o? Is anyone home in that lab coat?" I call out internally, rooting silently for my friend from the hall. Then, in an unprecedented move into ego, *so unlike* my friend, I hear him attempt to pull out his social pass card, "You know, when I am not in the hospital, I serve as (a socially and professionally important person)."

The internist remains impenetrable, not even feigning respect.

"Is that it?" I think. "We become old and naked, with nothing but a flimsy gown draped about a fragile frame, and we cease to exist as human beings? What if my friend had been a 'common' tradesman with no social card to pull in this game? What then?" My heart grows heavy at the thought.

Honor the Self in *everyone*.

335 Rest

Sometimes the most loving thing we can do for another person is to take on her morning duties and let her sleep.

JULIAN LYNN

336 Covenant

If we have entered successfully into a covenant of simple living with ourselves earlier in the year, the last month in our calendar becomes a delicious, uncluttered time of retrospection about the previous months, as well as a healthy anticipation for the year to come.

Yet, it is not too late. Regift or donate a few items; then, celebrate your new space and unfettered lightness.

337 Beyond Form

In a community affirming life, the common Thread is spiritual, connecting us all beneath the veneer of external, religious forms. Find common ground.

338 Receiving

    In the long holiday line at the post office, I pass the time with two joyful individuals. As we talk, some of my mind's overblown sense of seriousness and social obligation slip away and humor returns to my heart.

    Hours before, while in meditation, I had asked about where I needed to be in order to serve. Yet, here I am being served by these light-hearted souls.

    When volunteering to serve, it is important to stay open to the idea of receiving and being served. When we are aligned, Divine order forges the most extraordinary and timely of relationships for each of us.

    Listen. Let go. Live. Joy will visit.

JULIAN LYNN

339 Fantasy

Flipping through a glossy magazine to keep up with new faces and wor'dly concerns, I encounter a section devoted to what "the people" are buying—priced over-the-top shoes; outrageously expensive handbags; really-?-that-much-for coats; solidly pricey wrist bling; and, whatever.

Would it not be grand, if each such purchase were matched by a donation to a charity or foundation that actually digs wells for potable water; works to end food scarcity for children and adults around the globe; ensures the purity of food supplies; or, educates new parents on effective methods of raising children without abuse?

Would the world not become, quite suddenly, a changed place?

YOGA'S DEVOTIONAL LIGHT

340 Golden Key

Nestled in the context of each heart is an almost hidden door behind which Love resides. This door wants to be opened. To unearth its whereabouts, find a joyful activity, because laughter oils rusty hinges. A walk in nature will yield its key.

Meditation, in the wee hours of the morning, produces the salutation, "Now, open!" The Light within will grow to reveal the manner in which you should be loved. Love your Self, and a love for the Self in others will follow.

341 Believe

There is a place for you here.

JULIAN LYNN

342 Stories

    In the past, I did not shrink from offering candid, verbal snapshots from my life and the wealth of my experiences. The narrative arc of my life has been full.

    In sending and receiving stories, one thing I have learned is that not all of us hold parallel definitions or attitudes toward certain archetypes or social profiles. And, in creating social space for ourselves, we sometimes forget the dignity of our common humanity and our hearts.

    When a speaker divulges a narrative, it must go through the receiver's experiential and cultural filters. Quite often, if (and usually when) that "same" story comes out of the receiver's mouth, the sound clip is reworked or revised to the extent that the new version stands

YOGA'S DEVOTIONAL LIGHT

as a greater indicator of the current speaker's (initial receiver's) state of mind, emotional tone or cultural markers than an accurate representation of the story's original source or experience.

The next time you offer a story to someone or hear a story told, listen from an archetypal point of view. What part(s) do you play? How does another speaker cast herself in the telling of her own tale? Then, consider why.

In moving away from limiting and defined roles, as well as labels and others' notions, try choosing to become quieter and a more reliable listener. Finally, consider this question: How can story facilitate the entry into a relationship of integrity with Atman, within ourselves or when listening to someone else?

JULIAN LYNN

343 Mat Prayers

When T.K.V. Desikachar, a civil engineer by training and profession, returned home as an adult to study yoga with his father, Sri T. Krishnamacharya, (who is sometimes referred to as the grandfather of modern yoga), Desikachar reminded his father that he was not there "to be taught how to pray."

What Desikachar is referencing here, regarding prayer, is the ongoing, internal dialogue which occurs naturally during a dedicated practice. This dialogue and the relationship, between the I-maker and the Self, are both precious and sacred. An external "teacher" can only assist students by being true to her own internal dialogue. The practice, then, is to be true to yours. No one else can "teach you how to pray."

YOGA'S DEVOTIONAL LIGHT

344 Wisdom

Wisdom, more often than not, renders us quiet in social settings, as we listen for our current, personal truth.

Learning to remain quiet, before participating, prevents us from expounding another person's already spoken truth. Why not wait, listen and choose to speak your own?

345 Fred Astaire

Tip your hat to another's Perfection to refresh the perfect flower in your open heart and nourish the bud in another's. To achieve freedom, explore this practice in the sanctified space of meditation.

JULIAN LYNN

346 Entrainment

Entrainment occurs when an individual gives up her own breathing rhythm or pattern and takes on, or entrains with, the breathing pattern of another person.

Entrainment is a key teaching tool and concept used in Eastern spiritual traditions to grant students ease of access to certain emotional states, planes of consciousness or to facilitate the receipt of a teaching. Once we become aware of the concept, entrainment must be invited.

Because the true Teacher lives inside of each of us, we—as external guides or teachers—best assist our students by working to entrain with our own highest Light. Then, a student is more inclined to find the true Teacher—inside.

347 Baskets

Metaphorically, each of us carries a basket on our backs, where we receive flowers or stones from others, depending upon how they relate to us. And, from our basket, we cast rocks or blossoms into days, lives and baskets of others.

When visiting downward-facing dog, imagine dumping out those unnecessary rocks. Then, in upward-facing dog or cobra, weave the plethora of flowers around you into the very fibers of your metaphorical basket and Being.

348 After Yoga

Overcast outside, sunny on the inside.

JULIAN LYNN

349 Spiritual Gesture

After teaching a rigorous set of large classes, I go to renew my body at a local Indian restaurant. I had not been there in some time but was once a regular patron. Moving swiftly on autopilot, I want to grab a quick take-out tray of curry.

Striding purposefully into the Indian restaurant, fixated on my own physical nourishment, I witness in stunned amazement as a choreographed scene of three sari-clad women rise from their seats all at once, with their hands—fluttering like small birds in flight—taking prayer position at their hearts. They bow in genuine warmth, recognition and dignity to greet me. (The guest is King in Indian culture, especially villages.)

"Namaste," they proclaim in poetic chorus, like a group of dear relatives, whom I have not seen in a very long time. The sincerity behind this respectful gesture causes me to stop as I recall the reverential throngs in the film, *Gandhi*, bowing and greeting him on his salt march to the sea. That film scene, for me, best contextualizes this spiritual gesture.

"Namaste" is translated many ways: The Perfection in me sees the Perfection in you; The Light in me acknowledges the Light in you.

Certain language and gestures outside of their cultural context often lose the emotional depth, subtle nuances and impact they can have on the mending of the heart. Traveling in yoga circles for decades now, I have witnessed—with concern—as this deeply respectful word and gesture have been transformed into a pert curtsy, tumbling in an automatic manner over attendees at the end of an overly-packed, mainstream yoga class.

JULIAN LYNN

We, as Westerners, do not fully comprehend the reverential weight this acknowledgment possesses *until* we have had a sensitive, direct experience of its delivery from a sincere individual, who carries within himself the depth of cultural context that accompanies its full and meaningful usage.

As for myself, I know the day those women greeted me, my stride broke, my heart center reopened and my linguistic consciousness began the process of realigning to accommodate the protective umbrella this gesture has over the sacred Self. My personal delivery and use of both the word and gesture have become more thoughtful. Before I move or speak, I move solidly into the space of my heart.

Consider this the next time you give or receive this greeting or blessing. And, may we all work on becoming guardians of each culture's sacred gestures and speech.

YOGA'S DEVOTIONAL LIGHT

350 Challenges

Working with the body assists us in uncovering our inner strength. When we develop the ability to tap our physical strength, we learn how to apply our fortitude to other areas of our lives—whether facing professional, personal, ethical, creative or spiritual challenges.

Whatever our preferred practice is, and it will change with circumstances, it must honor our body and temperament, drawing us ever closer to essence.

351 Strength

Compassion is not a sign of weakness but a sign of profound, spiritual strength.

JULIAN LYNN

352 Signs

On my first day back, during a visit to the American Southwest, I bump directly into one of my former and most quietly devoted, community students.

Inquiring after her health, family and general well-being, she fills me in on her professional life and personal joys, finally, confessing that she has abandoned her hatha-yoga, mat practice.

The conversation ends with a stout verbal resolution on her part, "I am going to take our meeting and conversation as a sign that I need to get back to yoga."

Imagine your sudden appearance as a potential "sign" for someone else. What would you have your presence signify? What does your life represent?

353 Considerations

Tantrism teaches that, when employed appropriately, with balance and prudence, attentiveness toward our physicality may serve as a means of spiritual unfoldment. The path honoring the body as a sacred vessel involves experiencing physicality and our immediate community as a place of safety and, ideally, celebration on many levels—physically, mentally, emotionally, creatively, domestically and spiritually.

Caring for the frame, in patient, kind and tender ways, teaches us to extend respect toward the sanctity of another person's physical vehicle. Embracing such respect does not lead to debauchery or hedonism, but it can lead to our personal healing, as well as the extension of hope and physical support for the sacred vehicles of other incarnate souls.

JULIAN LYNN

354 Solstice

It is a sweet paradox: Winter officially begins as the sun commences broadening her warm grasp on our days.

355 Authentic

How may I serve another at the level of essence? This is one of the questions which may open the door to the Self within our own practice.

In answering this question during meditation, with patience and kindness, we move quickly through brief states of apparent "overindulgence" to fuel our Perfection in preparation for greater states of more expansive service and authentic living.

356 Intimacy & Love

So much is made of intimacy and love in the West. We fantasize and romanticize about finding that *one* person who will understand us, help lift us up and hold us physically as we explore what it means to be embodied.

But, the real, rarified intimacy we crave only comes about when we learn how to hold ourselves, talk ourselves up or down in stressful situations or listen to the cares of our hearts with tenderness, while attending to our physical needs with the same fastidiousness of a consistently loving grandparent. We must pursue positive inclinations toward the Self, as we would be inclined to pursue a new relationship.

If we are able to commit to this, we just might find ourselves falling in love.

JULIAN LYNN

357 Long-standing

Relationships are a practice, where we try to bring forth, in one another, our most luminescent gifts. Sometimes the more intimate and long-standing a relationship is the more difficult it is to maintain an open and forgiving heart.

Pull the close-up camera away from your partner, parent(s), child and your most intimate friends. Renew your internal vows to seek the fulfillment of your deepest, personal joys.

Then, after a space in time, bring your internal renewal forward, placing it consciously into your most long-standing and intimate relationships. Everyone, with whom you remain involved, will benefit from this renewal process.

YOGA'S DEVOTIONAL LIGHT

358 Responsibility

The concept of entrainment is a key teaching tool in many Eastern spiritual traditions. Entrainment is the release of one's own personal breathing rhythm for the breathing rhythm of another.

In yoga, historically, an aspirant would entrain with his guru until the point at which the student was ready to entrain with his own internal Teacher or Self. Ideally, entrainment is used to aid a student with his growth, spiritual maturation and, ultimately, upliftment.

Entrainment must be invited by the "lead" breather. And, it must be entered into wittingly and voluntarily by the person being invited to entrain.

Here is a sample class opening: "If it is appropriate, you are invited to exhale with me. Exhale out all that is not of your true

JULIAN LYNN

essence. And, then, on the inhaling breath, call all that is of your own pure Self into your body. As we practice today, listen to the wisdom of your body and breath, being mindful to take breaks according to your needs."

Uninvited forms of entrainment, performed wittingly, or the holding of students with statements such as, "You may only study with me," are wholly unrepresentative of what hatha yoga, in the West, is about—personal freedom.

Trust that students will sort themselves out until they find suitable matches for a time, place and teacher. It is better to encourage students to study with additional teachers than it is to attempt to hold students or limit your students' growth. Work to ensure that the sacred nature and integrity of yoga's many practices are maintained.

Become an ambassador for yoga.

YOGA'S DEVOTIONAL LIGHT

359 Letting Go

It is Christmas day. The streets are deserted. And, a house is being remodeled in our neighborhood on this quiet holiday.

As I walk the dogs past two hard-at-work, Spanish-speaking men, putting the finishing touches on some intricate stone masonry decorating the home's gigantic porch, I think to myself, "Maybe I could bring them some of the scones I just baked—something to help—something to celebrate the holiday."

Then, because I am fresh from my meditation practice and still plugged in, a response drops into my IN BOX, "If you truly want to help, go get your guitar."

This is more of a spontaneous gift than I had anticipated. But, walk home I did.

Most objects, when manufactured responsibly and with an awareness toward

JULIAN LYNN

the environment, are energetically neutral until we decide to do something with them. Thus, gifting this guitar would "improve" the objects luminosity from an energetic perspective. (Make sure that you are well grounded when following through on any gentle nudges you receive.)

So, fetch the guitar and hand it off I did. The guitar received an upgrade by being passed onto a person in need of a means of positive, creative musical expression. Believe.

360 Year's End

What an unbelievable year. It is amazing to *BE*. At home, we are enjoying freshly bathed dogs, listening to classical, Ravi-Shankar music and eating arils, edible gems, plucked from pomegranates, one of the world's most exquisite fruits.

361 Beauty

Beauty is not an external quality, though some may think it so, but an internal feeling and state of being in alignment with our Light and having that Light honored and respected.

Beauty is expressed when our own radiance filters through the body, most especially when someone loves and cares for us in consistent and kind ways or when we love and care for ourselves.

This is the observable truth.

Next time, while you are waiting to be seated at a restaurant, watch two people who are in love, as they interact. Light simply radiates from them, playing like the Northern Lights between two bodies.

JULIAN LYNN

362 Refuge

Through our dedication to our practice, it is not the world that changes, but we who change.

The seed of Stillness, buried in our hearts, becomes a place of refuge as we grow. There comes a point at which everything turns to color and Light.

Dedication to our practice removes masks of misperception, revealing the world's or another person's true nature and luminescent Perfection.

363 Gift

The work is so individual, private and rare that on some days it is difficult to be public, open and general.

364 Divine Intervention

From a conversation with a friend: Divine intervention comes when someone, who is in alignment and listening, responds to the request made by another's heartfelt and oft unknown longing. We sometimes witness Divine intervention when another attentive animal responds, in awareness, to the longing of a fellow creature's heart. In a broader sense, Divine intervention occurs when a group or individual responds to a call from one of the Earth's living systems.

What causes grief is how often we forget our sacred place and disregard our ability to respond appropriately to others in need, thereby losing the opportunity to touch another's life and heart.

In truth, Divine intervention, at its simplest, is attentive kindness.

JULIAN LYNN

365 Reverence

    Traveling by train, I find myself seated among an extended family from the Midwest, returning from a rare out-of-state trip to New Mexico. They are a family of professional farmers—the men—and teachers—the women—who left their large-scale, operation in the capable hands of hired managers to take a chance on a long trip of grand adventure.

    Sitting quietly in my seat while contemplating the return from my own solo travels, I meditate on the nature of relationship: Who am I? Who are you? What are we in relationship to one another? The invisible strands of love and care binding me to my adult child are still humming from our recent visit.

    Seated alongside this farming family, I overhear the negotiation of breaks having

YOGA'S DEVOTIONAL LIGHT

to do with the care of the youngest member of their party—the grandson/nephew/child. There is a tremendous respect and patience among them, made obvious by the way they handle even minor family transactions. They are *good people* by Midwestern standards, and the excitement they feel about their trip fills the compartment, helping us all feel more vibrant and alive.

Although I am quiet and looking out of the window, the excitement from their conversation begins to spill over into the space of my seat. At some point the mother of the young boy begins telling me about the details of their trip's itinerary, while flipping through a library's worth of photographs from New Mexico. Soon, we are looking at a group of photographs from the sanctuary of a venerable Roman Catholic Cathedral. Her tone changes from surprised excitement to reverential

JULIAN LYNN

respect as she shifts gears and enters into the space of her heart. It is at this time that a gentle inquiry is made regarding my own religious affiliation and identity.

These questions of religious affiliation and identity no longer surprise me because they have been asked so many times and by such a wide variety of people and in all manner of creative and imaginative ways. Yet, whatever the situation, the question of identity tends to come when the separation between "you" and "me" gives way to our Oneness, when our hearts link. The question attempts to verify whether or not it is safe for the other person to share candidly their most treasured and sacred, spiritual experiences.

My own spiritual heart, over the past many years of meditation, has been a territory of expanding Universality. Initially, like many individuals who have a meditation or devotional practice, I found myself sitting with some degree of old, unresolved pain, which would then be pushed aside to allow for bursts of incredible Stillness or Grace. Such experiences are what keep us revisiting our meditation practice and devotions.

After pain falls away, we may explore more freely the questions of the heart: Who am I? Why am I here? What may I do to help another's heart heal? Finally, our meditative sitting or contemplative practice of yoga's physical postures continues to teach us that connectedness—to the heart's inner sanctum—allows each of us to experience reverence. And, when we are careful to maintain an unbroken connection to that place of reverence, it becomes strong enough to carry over into the rough-and-tumble of our daily lives, through all manner of circumstances and during interactions with a wide variety of places and people.

JULIAN LYNN

Reverence, I have found, more than anything, is what we long for in the context of our relationships—whether those relationships are with aspects of our own personalities, with a variety of environments we find ourselves moving through or with one another.

When reverence is present, there is a natural desire, on the part of two people, to seek the potential commonalities of external identifiers. We begin asking this question: How are we alike—socially?

But, what if we moved beyond the impulse to name external commonalities and simply maintained the extraordinary connectedness to the inner sancta of our hearts? Then, false sheaths fall away, and reverence allows us to rest easily together, heart to heart, in one of the most fulfilling ways we may enjoy life's rich and varied bouquet. Peace to You.

YOGA'S DEVOTIONAL LIGHT

Recommended Resources

Desikachar, T.K.V. *The Heart of Yoga: Developing a Personal Practice*, Rochester, VT: Inner Traditions International, 1999.

Easwaran, Eknath, trans. *The Bhagavad Gita*, Petaluma, CA: Nilgiri Press, 1985.

_____ , trans. *The Upanishads*, Tomales, CA: Nilgiri Press, 2007.

Iyengar, B.K.S. *Light on Yoga*, New York, NY: Schocken Books, 1979.

Khalsa, Shakti Parwha. *Kundalini Yoga: The Flow of Eternal Power*, New York, NY: A Perigee Book, 1996.

Krishnamurti, Jiddu and D. Rajagopal, ed. *Think on These Things*, New York, NY: HarperPerennial, 1989.

Lasater, Judith. *Relax and Renew: Restful Yoga for Stressful Times*, Berkley, CA: Rodmell Press, 1995.

Prakash, Prem. *The Yoga of Spiritual Devotion: A Modern Translation of the Narada Bhakti Sutras*, Rochester, VT: Inner Traditions, 1998.

Rosen, Richard. *The Practice of Pranayama: An In-Depth Guide to the Yoga of Breath*, Shambhala Audio, Distributed by Random House, Inc., 2010.

S[h]ancarac[h]arya, Sri and Swami Madhavananda, *trans. Vivekacudamani (Crest-jewel of Discrimination)*, Calcutta, India: Advaita Ashrama, 1998.

Svoboda, Robert and Arnie Lade. *Tao and Dharma: Chinese Medicine and Ayurveda*, Twin Lakes, WI: Lotus Press, 1995.

Tiwari, Maya. *Ayurveda: A Life of Balance*, Rochester, VT: Healing Arts Press, 1995.

Yogananda, Paramahansa. *Autobiography of a Yogi*, Los Angeles, CA: Self-Realization Fellowship, 1998.

JULIAN LYNN

Index

A–C

abhinives[h]a, 129

ahamkara, 5, 107

ahimsa, 48, 51

alignment, iv, 37, 60, 112, 126, 172, 174, 180, 181, 229, 258, 279, 295, 305, 332, 361, 364

aparigraha, 63

appearances, 18, 88, 103, 182, 194, 205, 218, 244, 293

asana, ii, iii, vi, 89, 98, 119, 171, 238, 245, 274, 282, 291, 293, 301, 308, 316

asmita, 130

asteya, 57

Atman, iv, 5, 85, 130, 200, 281, 291, 293, 342, see Self

attachment, 124, 126 (raga)

attainments, ix, 172, 177, 184, 190, 207, see gifts

avidya, 24, 126

awareness, v, 3, 28, 52, 83, 88, 168, 171, 186, 193, 304, 359, 364

Ayurveda, 76, 327

bandhas, 98

Being, vi, 38, 42, 54, 78, 119, 158, 235, 248, 266, 281, 311, 323, 325, 347

bhakti yoga, v, vi, viii, ix, 42, 65, 108

bicycle(s), 96, 197, 272, 289

brahmac[h]arya, 60, see vital energy

Brahman, 234, 235, 237, 238, 265

breath regulation, iii, 32, 79 (pranayama)

Buddhism, 190

bus stop, 306

chakra(s), 301, 325, 349

charity, 165, 225, 244, 339

color(s), 21, 24, 41, 75, 125, 219, 258, 362

conceit, 96, 258, 321

consciousness, vi, 57, 97, 135, 145, 191, 196, 203, 208, 213, 224, 252, 255, 258, 265, 269, 274, 324, 329, 332, 346, 349

contentment, 31, 86 (samtos[h]a), 139

D-F

darshan, 249

Desikachar, vii, 190, 329, 343

devotion(al/s), v, vii, viii, 34, 37, 42, 45, 119, 164, 172, 180, 181, 289, 365

dharana, 254, 329

dharma, ix, 107, 180, 274

dhyana, 224, 329

disappearing, 184

Divine, v, ix, 4, 37, 41, 57, 60, 64, 77, 105, 112, 119, 126, 131, 142, 153, 172, 174, 180, 194, 211, 243, 258, 286, 312, 338, 364

Divine Mother, 152, 168, 227, 228, 244, 289

dream, i, 84, 103, 121, 130, 196, 199, 203, 237, 276, 314

dves[h]a, 127

Easwaran, viii, 265

ego, 23, 51, 124, 130 (asmita), 184, 214, 277, 334

elements, 204, 280

entrainment, 293, 346, 358

essence, 72, 155, 181, 222, 284, 312, 350, 355, 358

Eternity, 213, 318

faith, 70, 97, 119, 172, 227, 323

fear, 124, 129 (abhinives[h]a), 135, 176, 244, 309

forgive(ness), 23, 44, 92, 163, 164, 254, 275, 315

G-I

Gandhi, 207, 349

garden, 37, 59, 80, 81, 123, 133, 161, 202, 235, 237, 261, 271, 272, 285, 289

gift(s), vi, viii, x, 6, 20, 28, 30, 33, 34, 86, 95, 96, 103, 164, 172, 177, 181, 184, 187, 190, 193, 194, 196, 199, 201, 203, 204, 208, 222, 249, 272, 289, 313, 318, 330, 336, 357, 359, 363 giving, 57, 164 (bowl), 180, 289, 317, 328

God's party, 289

gossip, 44

Grace, 64, 135, 167, 173, 267, 273, 279, 365

gunas, 246

hatha yoga, iii, vi, 89, 100, 139, 274, 282, 291, 293, 304, 358

healing, v, 47, 76, 211, 214, 277, 309, 353

heat, 69, 89 (tapas)

Himalayan Institute, i, vii

Hinduism, 274

histories, 283

holiday(s), 1, 147, 183, 302, 303, 317, 320, 338, 359

homeless(ness), 37, 64, 96, 135, 150, 180, 194, 306

I-maker, 5, 107 (ahamkara), 343

intention(s), 47, 48, 54, 83, 113, 141, 164, 169, 200, 211

intuition, 286

is[h]varapranidhana, 95

Iyengar, iv, vii, 245, 301

J-L

jnana yoga, vi, 65, 274

karma, vi, 65, 297

kindness, 22, 118, 164, 169, 184, 236, 254, 272, 321, 326, 355, 364

Krishnamacharya, 343

Krishnamurti, vii, 1, 16

laughter, 10, 38, 215, 218, 306, 340

letting go, 359

levitation, 181

Light, x, 2, 32, 65, 72, 83, 107, 109, 132, 142, 167, 171, 182, 214, 222, 244, 251, 253, 258, 266, 269, 281, 286, 294, 297, 308, 309, 311, 315, 325, 340, 346, 349, 361, 362

Love, 25, 77, 92, 129, 144, 159, 181, 250, 262, 265, 268, 269, 289, 315, 329, 340, 356, 361, 365

M-O

mala, 257, 328

manifesting, 203

mantra, vi, 65, 122

marriage, 164

meditation, iii, v, viii, 5, 7, 32, 35, 37, 58, 64, 77, 79, 113, 115, 116, 119, 132, 135, 136, 150, 151, 158, 164, 167, 180, 186, 196, 211, 222, 224, 238, 242, 262, 269, 274, 277, 287, 289, 304, 308, 322, 324, 333, 338, 340, 345, 355, 359, 365

mind, 58, 64, 84, 89, 96, 107, 114, 156, 160, 171, 172, 192, 193 (reading), 194, 196, 198, 213, 223, 229, 231, 240, 251, 257, 258, 276, 291, 295, 304, 324, 329, 338, 342

misalignment, 305

misperception, 53, 124, 126 (avidya), 127, 129, 362

nadi(s), 217, 301, 325

namaste, 26, 175, 349

Narada, v, 108

narrative(s), viii, 5, 44, 93, 110, 138, 283, 192, 342

nidra, 191, 291

niyama(s), 83, 86, 89, 92, 95, see yama

noble travelers, 180

non-attachment,* 64, 201

non-harming,* 48, 51 (ahimsa)

non-possessiveness,* 63 (aparigraha)

non-stealing,* 57 (asteya)

Observer, 114, 165, 251, 284

old and naked, 334

Oneness, 121, 158, 365

P-R

past lives, 199

past/present/future (seeing of), 208

Patanjali, vii, 48, 231, 234, 235, 329

path, ii, vii, viii, x, 28, 34, 37, 48, 88, 89, 96, 107, 177, 184, 194, 196, 209, 256, 258, 269, 274, 277, 281, 286, 314, 318, 353

perception, 24, 44, 93, 110, 124, 129, 130, 145, 174, 247, 262, 272

play, 10, 107, 164, 187, 199, 202, 210, 214, 244, 263, 283, 290, 342, 361

Prakash, v, vii, 108

prana, 4, 102, 301, 310, 325, 327

pranayama, iii, 23, 32, 72, 238, 274

pratyahara, 101, 168, 239

prayer, 119, 194, 222, 257, 343, 349

Providence, 119, 180, 194, 211

purification, 69, 89

purity, 83, 141, 169, 232, 246, 339

raga, 126

raja yoga, vi, 65, 211, 304

Reality, 53, 88, 122, 129, 139, 152, 153, 205, 284, 300, 315

reject/refuse, 124, 127 (dves[h]a), 244

reverence, 42, 365

role(s), viii, 5, 95, 107, 141, 171, 187, 208, 244, 263, 283, 311, 342

*Hyphens were retained to match traditional texts and references.

S–U

Samadhi, 90, 228, 242, 293, see Union

samtos[h]a, 86

Sanatana Dharma, 274

Sanskrit, 27, 98, 107, 190

satya, 54

second sight, 222, 258

seed(s), 38, 85, 133, 258, 362

seers, 104

Self, iv, ix, x, 2, 5, 19, 20, 38, 46, 48, 50, 51, 60, 64, 67, 77, 79, 83, 107, 113, 114, 121, 130, 157, 158, 164, 171, 174, 186, 200, 204, 205, 206, 215, 233, 238, 248, 254, 258, 259, 267, 275, 278, 283, 286, 294, 297, 308, 312, 314, 319,

(Self) 324, 334, 340, 343, 349, 355, 356, 358

self-care, 51, 163, 296

self-study, 92

sense withdrawal, 101, 168, 239

s[h]auc[h]a, 83

Shankara, vii, 15, 228, 247, 284

sheaths, 158, 365

s[h]raddha, 97, 323

siddhi(s), ix, 172, 177, 190, 200, 204

single-pointed focus, 229, 254, 329

signs, 206, 352

sleep, 84, 121, 130, 170, 191, 215, 291, 314, 335

Spirit, ii, 50, 107, 128, 135, 144, 222, 266, 291, 295, 299, 321

spiritual gesture, 349

Stillness, i, iv, 23, 28, 32, 74, 88, 127, 179, 229, 233, 302, 320, 362, 365

stories, ix, 5, 44, 103, 110, 162, 180, 192, 260, 283, 342

surrender, 95 (is[h]varapranidhana), 148, 234, 238

sun(light), viii, 26, 30, 38, 40, 46, 55, 62, 72, 73, 81, 97, 119, 158, 178, 188, 193, 204, 221, 235, 237, 238, 271, 289, 290, 297, 318, 323, 348, 354

svadhyaya, 92

sweetness, 41

synchronicities, 60, 119

tantrism, 353

tapas, 69, 89

tattoo(s), 30, 64, 213, 299

teacher(s), ii, iv, 2, 102, 171, 177, 235, 258, 263, 284, 292, 343, 346, 358, 365

the frame, iii, 8, 39, 215, 248, 353

third-eye activity, 52

tree(s), 40, 56, 85, 143, 158, 272, 288

trust(ing), 39, 167, 171, 174, 211, 243, 277, 358

truth, 52, 54, 88, 113, 123, 139, 140, 171, 174, 196, 277, 326, 344, 361, 364

unconquered (by others), 201

Union, vi, 40, 65, 90, 115, 135, 155, 181, 215, 218, 242, 269, 274, 290, 304, 315, 324, see Samadhi

Upanishads, viii, 156, 158, 272

V-Z

Vedanta, iii, 153, 246, 265

vital energy, 54, 60 (brahmac[h]arya), 93, 134, 251

voice, 10, 30, 64, 67, 75, 96, 107, 240, 294, 306, 319, 324

weather, 55, 69, 75, 111, 135, 161, 178, 185, 189, 197, 200, 249, 259, 300, 315

wealth, 11 (bounty), 63, 146, 321, 332, 342

yama(s), 48, 51, 54, 57, 60, 63, see niyama

Acknowledgements

I would like to extend a deep and genuine gratitude to the hundreds of students, whom I served, allowing me to call the teaching of yoga and meditation my profession. And, to my clients, who grant me the privilege of working through the Light of their hearts with Pranic Work— thank you. Fulfilling another person's desires for an experience of the Self is always humbling. Your collective respect, inquisitiveness and honor focus a brighter understanding on Vedanta than any text, teacher or solo practice ever could.

These sentences are an insufficient expression of my heart-felt thanks for the anonymous individuals who appear in narratives supporting me through the process of living as a bhakti-yoga practitioner. Such a lifestyle is by no means a solo endeavor. Without the amazing and sacred stream of gracious souls who have aided me more than I have aided them, the support of my immediate and extended family, as well as regular extensions of Grace, there would be no work, no writing and no experiences to share. May peace be granted to you all.

    These acknowledgements would not be complete without another hearty bow before the Springfield-Green County Library District's many gifted and skilled reference librarians. Every one of you has worked with unflagging professionalism, patience and expertise with online assistance, finding rare, out-of-print books, which have long since passed through my library, as well as accessing the additional media which has sustained me through the creative process. I wish you all the best of health and happiness.

Julian Lynn, MFA, CEP, ERYT, has logged miles on her yoga mat and years on her meditation cushion. She spent five years in the American Southwest, living and teaching college-level and community-based courses in hatha yoga and meditation, as well as continuing to learn about life's beauty, vision and the importance of simply Being. Ms. Lynn offers personalized sessions in support of conscious living through certified energetic work or Pranic Work. It is a joy and privilege to serve individuals wishing to enhance and expand their experiences of the Self. She specializes in distance work. Please visit julianlynn.com for additional information.

www.ingramcontent.com/pod-product-compliance
Lightning Source LLC
Chambersburg PA
CBHW020731160426
43192CB00006B/187